To Juliet with

Jeany (Tracy)

LIFE AFTER DEATH
A Mother's Story

Jeany Pavett

Strategic Book Group

Copyright © 2010

Strategic Book Group
P.O. Box 333
Durham CT 06422
www.StrategicBookClub.com

ISBN: 978-1-60976-488-3

Printed in the United States of America

Book Design: Stacie Tingen

To my darling daughter, Gabrielle Jane,

You touched the hearts of many during your lifetime, most of all mine. This book is dedicated to you with all my love. You are gone but not forgotten. I carry you always in my heart.

For my wonderful husband, Donald, you have stood by me through thick and thin. How can I ever thank you? You have always been content to give me all the space and time I needed on my journey through life and to write this book. You have always been there supporting me in the background. You may think that everything you have done has gone unnoticed, but I hold it all in my heart and mind. The truth is – without you I would be nothing. You are my hero, the 'wind beneath my wings' and with your support I can fly, soaring on the wings of the eagle.

Through everything, you have stood by me, made me see the truth, brought so much joy into my life and turned all the wrongs to rights. You made my dreams all come true with the love that I found in you; for which I will always be thankful. You always hold me up and never let me fall; you have seen me through everything.

With you by my side I have wings to fly, and I feel as though I could reach the sky with your hand in mine. Each time I have lost my faith; you encouraged me and told me that nothing was out of my reach. With you I stand tall and having your love means that I have everything I need. I am so grateful for each and every day you have given me these past decades. The truth is that I have been blessed because of your love. You're the light in the dark, my inspiration and through all the lies of my life, you are the truth. I thank God that He brought us together; my world is a better place because of you. During all those times of my weakness you were my strength and when I couldn't find the words to speak, you were my voice. When I couldn't see the way anymore you, were my eyes to guide me.

Donald, I want to thank you for lifting me up, for giving me faith and believing in me. I'm everything I am because of your love for me. Thank you isn't enough, Donald, I love you, always have, always will.

All my love,

Jeany

xXx

For my beautiful and precious daughters, Megan & Elizabeth; you are my world and my life.

To the Special People over the years who have given me support and friendship to help me live.

To everyone who encouraged me to write this book; believed enough to give me the money I needed to get started, and prayed for me in this venture.

Thanks Peter for reading this book so many times and in offering encouragement and advice.

Mum – I love you more than you will ever know, thank you for being my Mum.

I thank God for you all. This is my story, the way I see it. The life I have lived.

Contents

Chapter 1

I'm Pregnant!

I felt quite strange and sort of all up in the air. I felt as though I was going to have appendicitis because I kept having a pain in my right side.

We had decided we would like to have a baby, but this was only the first month of 'trying' so I didn't dare dream that I could be pregnant.

I had terrible hunger pangs night and day, I felt I had to eat and I also felt as though my period was about to start. Donald was convinced that I was pregnant and kept talking to the 'baby'. He said he really had the feeling that he was going to be a daddy. I wanted to believe it, but tried to convince myself that I wasn't, so that I wouldn't be disappointed when my period did start. We had to wait until it was six weeks late before the doctor would do a test.

I became very emotional over the weekend, especially on the Sunday. I could not get the lid off the bottle of milk and when I did, my finger went through the lid and the milk splashed me and I almost cried about it. When I recounted the event to Donald – I did cry.

On the first of March I was in the kitchen preparing the tea when I heard a key turning in the lock and the front door burst open. Donald had just arrived home from work and he seemed very excited. "Look what I've got!" he waved a box in the air grinning – it was a home pregnancy test so that we didn't have to wait any longer than the morning for a result.

"But if I'm not pregnant, I'll be so upset; I don't think I can bear to do it."

"Well you supply the sample and I'll do the test!" Donald beamed.

Donald woke early; ushered me into the bathroom and fifteen minutes later swept me in his arms. "We're going to have a baby; we're going to have a baby!"

"Hold on, Donald, you didn't leave the test in the first compartment for ten minutes like the instruction said."

"Come on, Jeany, believe it, the line is there – clear as anything." Donald urged.

"Even so, I don't want to get too excited yet and be disappointed later." I replied.

"Okay, Jeany, we'll do the other test tomorrow morning to set your mind at rest if it will make you happier."

The next morning we did the second test and got another POSITIVE and I began to believe that I was pregnant, but we decided not to tell anyone until we had got the official doctors confirmation. We took a sample to the hospital then waited two or three days for the results to come back. I had wanted Donald to telephone for the result, but they said that it had to be me. The first time I telephoned it hadn't come back, but the second time it was there. Even though I knew that our tests were positive the 'official confirmation' bowled me over. I felt so excited and faint that the receptionist's voice faded away and I went into a sort of trance until I heard,

"Mrs Pavett, Mrs Pavett! Are you alright?"

"Yes, yes, I'm here. What do I do next?"

"We need to set a time for your first antenatal appointment; the clinic is on Tuesday's." The receptionist replied.

Appointment made, I telephoned the police station where Donald was on an early shift, to let him know. We were extremely happy. Our families were very excited too. This baby would be the first of a new generation on both sides.

I eagerly waited for the first trimester to pass so that we could begin to prepare for the baby's arrival. Naturally I worried about all the usual things that could go wrong and I was anxious for all the blood test results to come back; especially the one at sixteen weeks (AFP) to see if there was a chance of Spina bifida. When we found that it had come back with a raised level, it was cause for concern.

The Consultant I would be under had not yet started so I was in the care of the senior Obstetric Doctor filling in until the new one arrived. After my routine scan that everyone has at around sixteen weeks, we were told that we would have to see the Doctor in clinic the next day because the baby appeared to have a hernia.

When we arrived we were told that, in fact, the baby had an exomphalos, which meant that there was a hole in the abdominal wall and part of the gut was trapped outside. The Doctor told us that after the birth the baby would go to a London Hospital to have an operation to put it back inside. They were not concerned about the raised AFP level because after seeing the scan, the defect they found would explain the extra fluid – nature's way of protecting the baby. We were told that I would be regularly scanned to keep a close eye on the situation.

In June I had my first of my regular full structural scans which meant that every inch of the baby was looked at from head to toe by a Consultant Radiographer. Four weeks later I had the next one.

I was afraid in case the baby was in London for any length of time. What would I do with a baby in London and Donald at home? I felt torn already and nothing had happened yet. I was filled with panic and dread and that night needed to feel Donald's strong arms around me for comfort and support but he'd gone to work and wouldn't be home before two in the morning. I felt very isolated and afraid.

Donald had also fallen off the step-ladder in the baby's room and had hurt himself. How I wished he hadn't gone to work. I knew he would tell me not to worry until or if, we had cause to and that we should cross bridges as we came to them. I knew he was right, of course, but I still couldn't help it.

Not so long ago I had been thanking and praising God that our prayers had been answered and I had become pregnant very quickly unlike our parents who had taken some years to conceive and now I felt let down, confused. Why had this happened? What had I done? Why should my happiness be marred by a rare condition that no one had ever heard of? I prayed that it would not be a serious problem and that we would cope.

I remember the baby kicking me and wanting it to, but it felt eerie sometimes, knowing that there was another human being inside me. Once I actually felt its hand through my tummy. I could feel each finger; it must have had its hand spread out on the inside of my tummy pushing it upwards. It was wonderful. I loved this baby already with all my heart and I knew that my love could only grow stronger.

Chapter 2

The Stark Reality Learned

In August the new consultant arrived, "Welcome Mr. & Mrs. Pavett, come in and take a seat." His outstretched arm greeted us. "I've had your notes on my desk for a while and have been really looking forward to meeting you. I wanted to ask you, how much you knew about your baby's condition."

"Not a great deal, only that part of its gut is trapped outside its tummy and when it's born it will go up to London for an operation to fix the problem." I replied.

"Well there is a bit more to it than that, so what I'm going to suggest is that you go and see a Consultant Paediatrician who can explain everything there is to know about the condition, so that you are fully informed. How does that sound?" His soft Scottish accent was a comforting sound.

"That would be great, thank you. We'd rather be fully aware of what to expect than have a big shock when the baby is born – we want to know exactly what we will be facing."

The appointment to see the Paediatrician came through quickly, but we were not really prepared for what we heard. He explained that when a baby develops, the skin comes round from the back and closes at the front, leaving only the umbilical cord out. Occasionally, for some inexplicable reason, it goes wrong and the skin does not close properly. In our baby's case, according to the scans, the hole was in the abdominal wall and part of the gut had been trapped outside the stomach. In two-thirds of cases a straight forward operation is needed to put things back where they belong and close the hole. However, in one-third of cases there can be complications. Sometimes several operations are needed because there is so much gut and other organs (such as the liver) outside, that it would be impossible to put it all back in one operation. Sometimes there were kidney problems, heart problems and even Spina bifida, or the gut becomes twisted and, therefore, it could be damaged.

My scans had shown that the other organs appeared to be intact, but no one could say for sure what would be found until the baby was born. There had not been a case like this in our town for about four years because it was such a rare condition. All we could do was wait, hope and pray. The Consultant added that these babies also had a habit of arriving early – anything from twenty-eight weeks which could present more problems, because premature babies can have other complications.

As we left the hospital I clung to Donald,   "How do you feel now, Jeany?"

"I don't know," I choked, "like I've just got out of a boxing ring."

I was feeling very mixed up. I was pleased that we now knew what we were facing, but let down that I had got this far into the pregnancy without knowing the full situation. I was also very, very sad, hurt and upset that we had got a baby that had such a rare and serious condition.

I was already twenty-eight weeks into the pregnancy, so that very night I prepared my bags in case I went into labour.

We saw my Obstetrician again after we had been to see the Paediatric Consultant and he said that we probably knew far more than him about the condition now. He told us that I would have another scan in October when I would be thirty-seven weeks, to decide whether or not I would need a caesarean, unless I went into labour naturally in the meantime. He wanted to closely monitor the situation to be as prepared as possible for the birth of this special baby.

Chapter 3

Labour Begins Early

I was fed up and felt very strange. I was thirty-four weeks into the pregnancy. It was a beautiful sunny day and so I decided to wash the net curtains and windows while I had the time.

I noticed some clear discharge whenever I went to the toilet and decided to use pads because something was telling me that all was not well. I put my fears aside, however, and carried on.

The next day this discharge had become reddish brown so Donald telephoned the Saturday morning 'emergencies only' surgery and the doctor thought it necessary for me to go to see her straight away. She examined me and asked me lots of questions. "Well your blood pressure is slightly raised and with the pain in your side," she spoke thoughtfully, "I'd like to send you to the hospital. It could be the baby or it could just be constipation, I can't be sure, but bearing in mind the problems, I'd rather send you in." She telephoned the hospital and arranged for me to be admitted for observation. I was afraid.

Donald took me to the hospital and the nurses did more tests and examinations, then, strapped me to a machine to monitor the baby's heartbeat and whether or not there were any contractions. The heartbeat was fine, there were no contractions and the baby was now breach after being head down only a couple of weeks earlier. They decided to keep me in overnight for further observation. The midwife caring for me, while listening to the baby's heart beat, asked, "Do you have a preference for a boy or girl?"

"I'd like a little boy, but my husband Donald would choose a daughter; but most of all we both want everything to work out alright." I answered.

"Well, if I'm taking a guess," she replied cheerfully, "listening to the heart beat, I would say it's a little girl! I don't think you have anything to worry about today, sometimes G.P.'s panic."

All night there was banging, crashing, lights on, bleeping of machines – at last morning dawned. Once again tests were carried out and the heartbeat and contractions were monitored. There were still no contractions, but there was that beautiful sound of our baby's heart beating. I would have listened to it all day given half the chance!

My Consultant came to see me, he was such a gentleman. I was knitting mittens and bootees to take the baby home in, and as he approached my bedside, I put my knitting down. He said, "Carry on; I'll wait until you've finished your row!" Not many consultants would have said that on their busy rounds! I was touched. "All your tests have come back fine, so I think you can go home and get plenty of rest. Unless anything changes, we will stick with our original plan and I see you in my clinic in two weeks' time when we'll decide what course of action to take for the birth. The baby seems happy enough where it is at the moment."

Donald came and picked me up. We spent the afternoon watching films we had videoed, and then spent the evening next door with our neighbours, Faye & Owen to help eat some leftover food from their daughter's baptism that morning.

Monday morning came. Donald went back to work after having a few weeks off sick from an operation on his knee. His first shift back meant he had to get up at four forty-five that morning; I on the other hand, got up around eight-thirty. I had hardly noticed him getting up because I was so tired. I decided to clear up the kitchen so that everything sparkled and did some washing including all the baby's woollens ready for its arrival. At one o'clock, I went next door for tea and cakes with Faye.

Despite being up since four forty-five, when Donald got home around ten past two he quickly changed from police uniform into his old working clothes, loaded up the car with the junk from Faye's shed, then he and Faye went to the tip. This cleared the way ready for Donald and Owen to knock the wall down between the outside toilet and coal shed to make a utility room.

While they were out I minded their nine month old, Amy. I felt strange all day but couldn't put my finger on anything in particular so I didn't mention it. Owen cycled to work every day. Part of his route was through the park and so, to give us some exercise and fresh air, we decided that we would walk through the park to meet Owen. Owen and Donald discussed the best way to proceed with their demolition project!

Faye and I were beginning to get chilly as the evening air began to close in so when we got back home, Faye and I stayed indoors in the warm chatting while Donald and Owen went outside and began to sledge-hammer the wall down. Faye was preparing the dinner but the telephone kept on ringing with people wanting to know how Amy was after a fall she'd had on Sunday which had given her a black eye. The last time Faye was on the telephone Amy was sitting on the kitchen worktop and I was watching her to make sure that she didn't fall off.

I suddenly felt as though I had started to wet myself. I couldn't go to the toilet because I didn't feel as though I could lift Amy off the worktop so waited until Faye had finished on the telephone. I had the feeling that something wasn't quite right. So as soon as Faye had finished the call and had taken Amy, I went up to the toilet.

As Faye called the men in for dinner, I walked towards Amy in the lounge to give her a bottle – again, I felt a little water drain from me. As soon as Donald came in I asked him to give Amy her bottle so that I could nip home and take my medicine for the indigestion the baby was causing me by pushing upwards onto my stomach due to its breech position.

I walked through my front door and water poured out from me. I went up to the toilet and still more came out. I changed my clothes and put on a pad. My body began to shake uncontrollably I didn't know if I was hot or cold or what I wanted to do. I went back next door where Faye had just dished up the dinner and poured out a glass of wine each. I announced, "Either I have wet myself or my waters have just broken!" My words hung in the air for what seemed like an eternity.

I went up to Donald and he held me. I became more afraid and had to fight back the tears that were welling up inside me. Faye ran next door and packed me a bag – I had emptied it all out to wash the things after my stay in hospital over the weekend. While she was there the telephone rang.

It was Donald's mum. Faye quickly explained that I was being taken into hospital. She had been unsure whether or not to answer it, either way Donald's mum would have been worried.

Donald called the hospital and then an ambulance while I lay down on the sofa feeling silly and afraid of what was probably about to happen. Just as the ambulance pulled up, neighbours from over the road came across, which made me feel even worse because that meant there were more people to see my vulnerability since the traumas in my childhood. I just wanted to be left alone.

Donald came in the ambulance with me as Owen said he would pick him up from the hospital when he needed to come back home. My body shook uncontrollably as I lay on the stretcher. The ambulance man was a happy chap and, with his cheery banter, tried to take my mind off the terrifying situation I found myself in. His face was one big smile as he asked me lots of questions and when I said that I had no pains he said, "Good! That makes my job easier!" and smiled. "Do you have a name for your baby?"

"Yes, we've had names for months, Michael Paul for a boy and Gabrielle Jane if it's a girl." I replied.

"Well, my name is Michael – so that's a good choice for a boy!" he exclaimed. Michael kept chatting to me all the way to the hospital, but try as he might to be positive, my mind was racing with so many thoughts and fears.

When we got to the hospital, I was taken to the labour ward, put in a room on my own, rigged up to the monitors and internally examined. I was only two centimetres dilated and my waters had not completely gone – apparently it was only my back waters trickling – it seemed more like a flood to me! My Consultant was telephoned and he told them that I would need to have a caesarean section if I went into labour. He asked to be kept informed of the situation and he would come in when needed. There were three reasons for a caesarean:

1. The baby was breach,
2. We had this exomphalos/gastroschisis to consider,
3. I was only 34 weeks pregnant.

A section would give the baby the best possible chance of survival. The gut could get damaged on the way out through the birth canal whereas if I was cut open they could take precautions to stop any further damage.

My contractions did start and I had a terrible backache. I was in a state of panic. "It's too early! It can't come yet!" I cried over and over again. The midwife did her best to try to reassure me. I felt sorry for Donald because he had been up since four forty-five, had an eight hour shift at work, taken a car load of rubbish to the tip, walked to the park to meet Owen with us, and then had been doing lots of strenuous work all afternoon – now this!

My contractions got worse, stronger and more frequent. The midwife called the duty doctor, a large, foreboding lady, who said that I ought to be prepared for theatre. I was shaved and had to have some oral medication, a

11

pre-med. I was to have some more of this medicine on the way to theatre. When I was ready for theatre, the duty doctor came back in to see me but rather than take me straight to theatre, she decided to give me another internal examination, her presence in the room filled me with terror. She waited until I was in the middle of a contraction before thrusting her hand inside me. It was an excruciating examination and she was very rough. At the end of it she announced, "You still haven't dilated beyond the two centimetres so I'm not going to take you to theatre after all."

Anger welled inside me, "It's not coming out that way so what does it matter if I haven't dilated?"

She ignored me and as she left the room, she called over her shoulder, "You'd best get some sleep!"

I am convinced that she didn't want to perform the operation herself because of all the complications but equally she didn't want to call my Consultant in.

Donald tried to doze in the chair beside my bed. I was in agony and I couldn't have any pain relief whatsoever and to make matters worse I was so dry and dehydrated and yet I couldn't even have a drink. But my thoughts turned to Donald. I couldn't imagine how tired he must be after his long day. Our plans for a lovely meal with friends, followed by a relaxing bath before going to bed had long since disappeared. I looked at Donald. His head lay on his arms which rested on my bed and I stroked his hair. It felt stiff and dry. Pieces of brick and brick dust crumbed between my fingers and emphasised my thirst.

I hadn't wanted anyone to know when I went into labour, but we felt that Donald had to telephone our families to let them know that I was in hospital and a caesarean was planned. I knew that they would be waiting for news all-night and so would not settle.

Throughout the night the midwife kept peeping round the door to see me and obviously thought I was asleep as that is what was written in my notes. How could I possibly have been asleep with everything that was happening to me?

At nine o'clock in the morning, my Consultant appeared cheerfully at my side. He took me for another scan to be sure of the exact position of the baby which was all very well, but it meant that I had an uncomfortable trip. The Labour Ward was on the third floor in the main block of the hospital. I was put in a wheelchair and taken to the lifts. Once on the ground floor I was wheeled out into the morning air. Initially it seemed refreshing but then I began to shiver as the cool air breezed through me as I began the bumpy ride across the car park toward the Antenatal Clinic building where the scan could take place.

As the building loomed closer, my mind raced. I knew that it would be filled with pregnant ladies who would be happy and looking forward to seeing their baby on the scan. Not so very long ago I was one of those ladies with everything to look forward to. Not now. Not today. Today I felt I had to put on a brave face and smile because I didn't want to cause the pregnant ladies any distress, but inside I felt as though I was about to lose everything.

I was wheeled into the scanning room and had to climb on the bed from the wheelchair which was extremely difficult and painful. The contractions were very frequent, more unbearable, and my back was absolutely killing me. I then of course, had the reverse journey back to the labour ward.

Eventually they decided to prepare me for the caesarean, but then my Consultant had another idea. He wanted to see if they had a space in another hospital where I would be able to have the caesarean and the baby would be able to stay with me. I was passed caring; I just wanted to get it all over with. My body; racked with increasing pain for the last fourteen hours or so was so very tired. I didn't care about anything except getting rid of the pain as soon as possible.

There were no spare beds at that hospital, so my Consultant said that he'd have to perform the caesarean here and send the baby to the London hospital as originally planned. They had been warned that a "Special Baby" was to be delivered very soon and so they were waiting for the birth to be confirmed and then all the arrangements could be made to transfer the baby to them.

"In the meantime, is there anything I can do for you?" he smiled.

"Get rid of this back pain!" I snapped,

"I can do that for you." He cheerfully replied and disappeared out of the room.

I lost count of the number of people who came to see me in preparation for the operation, one of the nurses tried to make me smile by telling me that all the men in theatre would be wearing gowns because they had run out of trousers – it didn't work! I suppose she meant well but I couldn't have been less interested.

Chapter 4

Meet Gabrielle

At last, at ten thirty, approximately fifteen hours after my contractions had started, I was given some more pre-med and wheeled down to the theatre. I hadn't eaten for about twenty-one hours and hadn't had a drink for at least seventeen. I was tired, hungry, in agony and couldn't wait to be put to sleep. The nurse told me to say goodbye to Donald, but whisked me backward in to theatre before I had the chance to even drawer breath to speak.

I wasn't prepared for what I saw when I went through the doors. No preparation room, I was directly in the theatre. It was crowded. There was a team of doctors and nurses for me, another team for the baby and students to watch and learn. I was told to get on to the operating table. "You'll have to wait until my contraction has passed." I snapped.

No one helped me. A sea of masked faces with gloved hands held out in front of them filled the room and yet I had to climb on to the operating table by myself. A smiling voice from behind one of the masks filled the air, "Do you remember me and what I said about the gowns?"

"I remember you said it." I muttered as I lay down on the operating table. Without warning it moved and frightened, me. It seemed to tilt sideways tipping me on to my left and I thought I was going to fall off! My Consultant came in, "Don't worry it will all soon be over."

I looked at the wall clock. It was ten fifty. At last I was given the anaesthetic. My eyes closed.

According to my notes this is how the next ten minutes went: -

"1055 – Knife to skin

1100 – A live female infant was lifted from the womb with a good APGAR score, and a good pair of lungs!" The APGAR score is a measurement of a newborn's response to birth and life outside the womb. Ratings are based on the following factors: Appearance (colour); Pulse, Grimace (reflex), Activity and Respiration. A high score is ten and the low end is one. She was immediately taken to the Special Care Baby Unit.

Though I didn't know it at this point, on Tuesday 27th September, Gabrielle Jane had entered the world weighing four pounds, thirteen ounces and she was eighteen inches long.

I gradually began to come round from the anaesthetic and was aware of a nurse by my side holding my hand. "Hi, my name's Chris and I'll be looking after you today." She said kindly.

"Where's Donald?" I croaked.

"He's at the Special Care Baby Unit with your baby."

"Is it alright?" I asked.

"She's fine," Chris replied.

"So it's a girl then." I mumbled, "Donald will be pleased."

I dozed off again. All I wanted to do was sleep and everything around me was a haze. What I was fully aware of though, was that I no longer had the pain and that was fantastic. I was also aware that Chris was by my side constantly.

When Donald came to me I woke again. Chris left us alone. He took my hands in his. "The midwives gave me some Polaroid photographs of Gabrielle so that you can have them."

"What's she like?" I croaked.

"She's beautiful. When they came out of the operating theatre to tell me that she has been born, I cried. A nurse took me to the Special Care Unit so that I could see her. I've spoken to our parents. It was difficult to get hold of my Mum because she had already gone to work, but I got her in the end. They all send their love."

"I want to see her." I choked.

"I've asked them. They're just getting her ready to go to London at the moment. I'll be going with her." Donald tried to reassure me, "Faye's going to bring me some food to take with me."

"Make sure that you don't let her out of your sight. I don't want them to get her mixed up and give her to someone else." I panicked.

"Don't worry. I'll be there."

"I want to see her." I wailed.

"I'll go and ask again." Donald left me to find someone to bring Gabrielle to me.

When Chris came back she saw that I was distressed,

"I want to see my baby," I cried. "I want to see her!"

"I'll go and find out what's happening." she said. Chris was a lovely young girl, an Australian who had come here to train as a nurse.

Eventually Gabrielle was ready to go to London; they brought her up to me in a mobile incubator and placed her on the bed beside me. I hugged her as best as I could. I didn't want all those people around me; I wanted to be alone with her. "I love you darling, Mummy's Angel. Please don't die before I get to come to see you and hold you properly." Her eyes were closed, she was sleeping peacefully.

All too quickly, the nurse took Gabrielle away from me and put her back in the incubator. Donald kissed me goodbye and off they went. I felt gutted, so very alone, upset and exhausted but I was too emotional and tired to cry. I went back to sleep again.

Chapter 5

A Childhood Dies

When I was eleven, my Mum and stepfather decided that I should learn about the facts of life before I went up to secondary school so that I wasn't ignorant. The thing was, I already knew enough and I didn't feel comfortable discussing it with them. My Mum was incredibly embarrassed and never liked talking about such things, so she didn't stay for the entire conversation, preferring to leave it to my stepfather. I dutifully asked a couple of questions so as to give the impression that I didn't know it all and then went off to bed.

A few days later my stepfather woke me at around six o'clock and told me to go downstairs to make a cup of tea for my Mum while he got ready for work. It was a struggle to get out of bed but I did and went down to the kitchen. The second I reached the kitchen I was struck with fear, I wanted to run away, panic rose from inside up to my throat and I felt as though I would choke and yet, I didn't know why. I walked toward the kettle. "It's okay, I've already put it on." he said.

I could see that the tea was already prepared; panic like the lava in a volcano, began to rise inside me and terror struck me rigid as he asked, "You know that sperm we were talking about the other night, do you want to see it?"

"Not really," I answered as unenthusiastically as I could.

He drew me close to his side and undid his trousers. I was petrified. He put one of my arms around him, took out his penis, placed my other hand on it, held it there and began to masturbate. He took his hand away so I removed mine. He put my hand back again, held it there and carried on masturbating. He kept taking his hand away because he wanted me to

18

masturbate him to a climax, but each time he let go, so did I. Eventually he held my hand in place and didn't stop until he spilled his semen onto the kitchen floor. He guided me to the sink. He shoved my hand under the tap. Mopped the floor then told me to take the tea up to my Mum!

I was thrown aside like a used oily rag. I didn't know how to react, what to do, where to go. I cannot adequately describe the feelings I had. It was surreal and I just couldn't comprehend what had happened. I felt used, powerless, sick, terribly afraid and so very alone.

I took my Mum her tea and got back into bed. I had nowhere to turn, no one to talk to, and above all, no one to rescue me. I couldn't tell my Mum, because she wouldn't listen.

When I was six years old, I came home from school to see my Dad's car parked outside our house. My sisters were playing on the driveway and my Mum was leaning into the car and I thought she was talking to my Dad. I felt happy, my heart skipped a beat seeing my Dad home, I was filled with anticipation of what delights were in store. I was a real "Daddy's Girl"; I loved to spend time with my Dad.

I remember one day I was sitting at the table and my nose started to run, I must have been about four at the time. I was in a panic not knowing what to do, I called out, "My nose is running! My nose is running!"

Dad immediately rushed to me, scooped me up from my chair and held me under my arms in front of him and ran me around the kitchen, saying; "Run after it then! Run after it. Come on, haven't you caught it yet?" I remember giggling like crazy as my little legs barely touched the ground. It's a memory that will always make me smile.

But this day, as I neared our home, I could hear something different. My Mum was not talking as I had suspected but sobbing, I was to learn a few minutes later Dad was leaving home. He'd found happiness with our next door neighbour's wife. 'Daddy's Girl' had lost her Daddy.

My Mum's world had shattered in a thousand pieces. She was distraught and wouldn't eat. I remember trying to snap her out of it by saying that if she wasn't going to eat, then neither would I! My Mum had been rejected for a younger woman, she was devastated and her world had fallen apart and she didn't know what to do. She begged my Dad to come back but he wouldn't. Mum needed a man in her life no matter what, alone she couldn't cope.

Chapter 6

Abuse, Fear and Abandonment

I was six years old when we moved from the north to live with my Mum's parents in the south. I don't remember much about it but do remember that it took a very long time. One of the trains had a corridor and I remember walking along it clutching my stuffed dog. When our journey came to an end, we got in a black taxi-cab which took us to my Grandparents house where we stayed for two years until my Mum remarried.

In contrast to the life I remembered with my Dad, my Grandad was a very strict Victorian man and ruled with a rod of iron. Shocked, I watched him slap my Mum, she was sitting on the arm of the chair crying, but I had no idea why he did it.

A man of rigorous routine, my Grandad always had to watch the tea time news; a time in which he expected total silence. My Mum would take us up to bed out of the way and read us stories; it was a special time with Mum. She did it because it was easier for all of us for the sake of peace and quiet. My Mum did what she had to do to keep my Grandad appeased; it meant that we were being looked after and she didn't have to cope alone.

We did have some good times there though, especially quality time with Mum. I remember going to the local newsagent shop and we had races back home. I laughed as we ran gleefully along the road. Mum ran ahead of me, I caught up and overtook her, the first to reach my Grandparents driveway.

I only have a few memories of living with my grandparents one of which was that I found it too traumatic to go to school. I had settled into my first school well, made lots of friends and enjoyed myself there until that day I walked home to find Dad leaving. I was given permission to stay off for the rest of the school term, but after Christmas the dreaded day arrived.

Mum took me to the school office and then left. I screamed and cried, absolutely distraught at being abandoned. As soon as the office lady turned away from me, I opened the door and ran out of the room, and the school, to chase after my Mum. The first my Mum knew about it was when a lady stopped her, "Is that little girl with you?" She enquired.

Mum turned and saw me. "Jeany, what are you doing?" She exclaimed. "You should be in school."

Mum took me by the hand and walked me back to school. This time I saw the lady turn the lock in the office door. I just wanted to be with my Mum, I was petrified that I would go home from school and find Mum leaving me just as had happened with my Dad a short while ago. The ladies at the school calmed me down and gave me a few books to read; I was allowed to ring the bell for the break times and "helped" by doing jobs.

Over a period of time I was introduced to my teacher and class mates little by little and eventually staying in the classroom on a full time basis. I began to realise that school wasn't so bad after all and began to grow in confidence that my Mum would still be there when I got home.

At home, my Grandad used to go to bed earlier than both my Mum and Nana because he had to get up early in the mornings for work. Grandad was a dustman, except if we told anyone this, he would snap indignantly, "No I am not I only drive the dustcart!"

One night I woke up to find that he was standing over me, he was holding my hand on something, I didn't understand or know what it was, but I knew that it felt wrong. Each night I would lie awake waiting for him to come into the room so that I could hold my hands tightly under the covers. He eventually got fed up with trying to get one of my hands out from under the covers, and to my dismay and guilt he moved to my sister, who

22

"top and tailed" the bed with me. This was when I started to learn to shut down and shut out from what was going on.

One night when my Mum came up to bed and I started to try to talk to her about what was happening. "What are you doing awake at this time of night?" She wondered.

"Grandad comes in here when you and Nana are downstairs."

"He probably comes to see you are alright." replied my Mum, hesitantly.

"No." I answered, "He makes me hold his finger!"

A wave of icy cold fear crossed the room and turned to ice that showed in my Mum's actions.

Even at such a young age, I could sense her fear and panic as she muttered something I couldn't understand and got into bed. Even though I was somewhere between six and seven years old and didn't know what it was that my Grandad made me hold, I knew it was wrong. So you can see now, why I couldn't tell her about my stepfather.

For the years up to when I was eighteen my stepfather abused me in every way, physically, sexually and emotionally. One day my Mum called me from upstairs and like most teenagers I said that I was coming but never did. I thought that my own time was good enough and so I carried on with whatever it was I was doing. Before I knew it, I felt as though I'd been hit by an express train at full speed; the back of my head was reeling. My stepfather was behind me; he grabbed hold of me, turned me around and threw me out into the hallway from the dining room.

"When your mother calls you, you come straight away and not when you feel like it!" he raged.

As he shouted this he was like a bull that charges the cape, he continued to come after me. As he threw me into the hall I fell to the ground which angered him even more – the atmosphere was on fire.

He grabbed the back of my trousers with one hand, the scruff of my neck with the other to try to pick me up, but my trousers ripped resulting in me falling back to the ground and he was left with ripped material in his hands. He kicked me down the hall, then punched and kicked me up the stairs to where my Mum was waiting. I don't even remember what she wanted me for.

That was one of many beatings.

My Mum sometimes begged him to stop, but he would almost hit her for interfering. Although I never saw him actually hit her, this was the one woman who showed me love and so I would have done anything to step in and stop him from hurting my Mum.

Our relationship became a battle and that no matter how I felt, I would never cry. I would not let him see he had won. The more he beat me, the stronger I became and I refused ever to cry. So the result was he beat me more. A vicious circle of events developed until in sheer frustration he would banish me from his sight.

I shared a room with my sisters, and if they were in our room when I got there, the conversation was always the same. "You ok?" one of my sisters enquired.

"Fine," I replied, "One day I'll hit the bastard back."

On the rare occasion I found myself alone, it took all my strength to hold back the tears. If a few escaped I would quickly check them just in case my stepfather appeared. I was frightened to let him see any emotion from me at all. I didn't want him to have any satisfaction or to ever think that he had succeeded in his endeavour to break and hurt me. I also didn't want to appear weak.

My stepfather never once threatened me not to tell anyone. He didn't need to; the emotional shackles were so strong. He further threatened that as we were so naughty we would each be sent to separate children's homes and he'd make sure we never saw each other ever again. My Dad had left us and I'd not seen him since, so the last thing I wanted was to lose my Mum and sisters as well. By now I also had little brothers toddling around whom I adored; I didn't want to ever be separated from them either.

He took every opportunity to engineer the situation to get me alone with him. My Mum had a knitting machine in the dining room and was struggling to get a particular part to work. My stepfather and I were trying to help her. When he judged the time was right, he turned to my Mum, "You look tired love, why don't you go to bed – Jeany and I will sort it out for you."

That same feeling that I had when I tried to talk to my Mum about my Grandad quickly travelled across the room. It was like a cover being pulled over a swimming pool but this time with me underneath it. I knew what would happen as soon as my Mum was safely upstairs and there was absolutely nothing I could do to change it.

Another ruse he regularly came up with was when he liked to take a bath. He'd announce that he was going up and would soon be ready for his back to be washed. My Mum would send me to him. Whenever I took a bath, I was forbidden by him to lock the door. My stepfather would come in to teach me the best way to "wash myself".

I also wasn't allowed to close the bedroom door which enabled my stepfather to come in whenever he wanted to. I would often be aware of him standing and watching me. At night he would come to the bedroom to say goodnight. Even with four of us in my room and my sisters in their beds he'd put his hands under my covers to touch me intimately.

Trips out in the car were not safe. Every time I was alone with my stepfather there was the chance that he would abuse me.

I did, however, have one room in the house that didn't involve sexual abuse. It was the downstairs toilet and it became my sanctuary and haven.

One day the ultimate betrayal happened. My pregnant Mum had gone to look after her Mother and had taken the boys with her. My sisters were in bed and I was left alone in the lounge with my stepfather. I could feel the tension and was frightened at what might happen. I forced a stretch and yawn and said that I was tired so would go to bed. He stopped me and in a gentle voice said, "Do you remember when I used to work away and you used to sleep with your Mum...."

I started to switch off fearing what was going to happen. His voice began to fade into the background, and darkness enveloped me like a shroud.

When he and my Mum were first married my stepfather would often work away from home. At those times I would stay up late with my Mum watching television and when it came to bed time I would sleep with my Mum. I loved those times so much and looked forward to snuggling up with my Mum – they were such special times and I was always disappointed when it was time for my stepfather to come home as I would have to go into my own bed.

I must have been around nine years old at the time he was referring to. "...........and one day you said to me that........" His voice echoed around me, it was far away and yet on top of me. Immobilised I heard, ".......you'd like to sleep with me? Well now's your chance!" and he began to lead me upstairs.

"I don't remember saying that." I lied. I had said it but he had taken it out of context so now I only had myself to blame. He must have been planning this for many years. I tried to plan a means of escape, "It's okay thanks," I blurted out, "I'll just go up to the bathroom then go to my own bed."

He waited outside the bathroom door and led me by the hand to their bedroom. As I lay there, I brought down the shutters. He was heavy, at about five feet ten inches tall and I would guess somewhere around thirteen stone. He was much bigger than my twelve year old frame, and I felt suffocated and claustrophobic. There I was, in my Mum's bed, buried underneath my stepfather. He prised open my legs and was pressing himself between them. Of course, he had decreed that I could never wear underwear in bed always being told that it was unhealthy and so I could feel his nakedness on mine. I began to freak out and was rigid with fear. I turned my head away from him when he tried to kiss my lips. I blocked out who I was and the situation I found myself in. I bolted the shutters firmly closed.

On the odd occasion when I refused to go out with him or stay up with him, my Mum would have a word with me the next day. Typically she would say, "You really upset your father when you wouldn't go out with him last night." Could she not see what was happening? Why would she not see how distressed I was?

I remember holidays were not exempt either. There was one particular occasion on holiday that stuck in my mind. We went to the beach. My stepfather wanted to hire a raft but no one else wanted to go out on one with him. My Mum encouraged me to go with him, I didn't really want to but thought that there couldn't be any harm in it; after all, we were in a public place.

We began walking out to sea with it until we got deep enough to swim, pushing it a bit further out. This was a prime opportunity for my stepfather to begin to put his hand inside my bikini bottoms and touch me. As quickly as I could, I pulled myself up on to the top of the raft and waved smiling to my family on the beach. Why did I keep on feeling the need to show everyone that everything was okay?

There were so many occasions that the abuse happened. Sometimes it seemed to stop and I was lulled into a false sense of relief and security, however, these times were short lived and it soon started up again.

I always tried to imagine that I wasn't there, but he would talk to me and ask questions which made it harder to distance myself. He had the need to convince himself that he was giving me pleasure and so his questions were often, "Do you like that?" "Is that nice?" I just didn't know how to react or what to do for the best and could never get away from his vice like grip. I didn't like him asking me questions because it made it harder for me 'not to be there'. I gave him answers I thought he wanted to hear.

On one occasion, early in the abuse, we were in the kitchen "making my Mum her early morning cup of tea" and my stepfather was touching me and I had a brilliant idea. Every time he touched me I felt ashamed as if somehow all this was my fault. My mind raced for a way to bring it to an end and I remembered that I often fainted for no apparent reason, so I said, "I don't feel well. I've gone all dizzy."

I heard him say, "You'd better go back up to bed then."

It had worked! Off I went, elated that I had managed to get away. But that wasn't the end of it. He came to me later in the day and said, "You know you felt dizzy earlier? Well that was probably the feeling I was trying to show you."

I felt crushed and wanted to vomit. Dizziness was an excuse, I didn't really feel dizzy but I'd said the wrong thing, now he seemed really proud of himself and I was more ashamed than ever. I didn't see my stepfather as an abuser. I didn't know there was such a thing. I knew that he had a temper and the slightest thing would set it off so all I wanted to do was please him. There was one occasion when a programme came on the television about incest, and he had made me turn the television off, but I didn't understand what it was.

One day he asked me if I ever touched myself, to be honest it was the last thing I'd ever thought about doing, but I knew what answer he wanted so I said, "Yes."

"That must be the banging noises I can hear when you are bed. If that's the case I'll excuse it."

I had absolutely no idea what "banging noises" he was on about, because as far as I was concerned there weren't any. It gave him another kick to think that I was masturbating in my bed while he sat in the lounge underneath me, watching the television. Just the thought of that made me feel defiled once again; I could never cleanse myself of him.

In future when he asked me questions as to whether or not I liked what he was doing I would just answer, "It's alright." It wasn't alright, it was far from alright, I was feeling guilty, humiliated, filthy, used, frightened. I felt sick to my stomach and my heart was as heavy as a stone. The way I coped was to blank my mind so that I didn't have to be there. I imagined I was somewhere else, that this person my stepfather was 'teaching sexual activity' to, wasn't me – I was somewhere else – anywhere – but not there.

The mental torture also had sexual intonations to it. Once he showed me a necklace and asked,

"Do you think your Mum would like this? I got it for her for Christmas."

"Yes. I'm sure she will." It was a cute little Panda with a pearl clasped between its paws.

On my birthday, which is near Christmas, I opened a present from my parents. It was the necklace. Shocked I muttered, "Oh. Err, thanks."

My stepfather waved his arms about and walked out of the room saying, "You are so ungrateful and if I gave you a million pounds you'd just say 'Oh thanks' or 'It's alright.'"

He wasn't, of course, referring to the gift. The suit of armour I lived in weighed heavy. As the eldest of six, I was given responsibilities. I babysat, did housework and cooked meals. I sometimes objected, but there wasn't much point. Whatever I did was never enough. There was always something more I should have done. I was constantly striving to achieve perfection, to prove I could do what they wanted me to do, in the hope that I would be that perfect daughter and earn proper respect and love.

I didn't have many real friends. Even the ones I made only seemed to tolerate my company. I was the one left behind when they went to the cinema or into town, the one who never got chosen at school by classmates, I got left until last and usually ended up being paired with those who were the least able. I was ridiculed, teased and bullied. I didn't enjoy school but got on with my work and studied as hard as I could and was very much alone.

The time came for me to choose my options at school and I felt that, as I was good at languages, I should look to a career where I could use them. "I'd like to be an Air Hostess when I leave school." I announced one evening around the dinner table.

"You don't want to do that," sneered my stepfather, "they only want pretty girls, and besides, it's a short life!" His words like a knife cut me in two, he might just as well have said, "You can't be an Air Hostess, you're far too ugly!" But I pressed on,

"Why? Is it because you get killed in a plane crash?"

"No, it's because once you get to a certain age they don't want you anymore! What you really want to be is a Bi-lingual Secretary, because it would be a good career, for a single woman and, you can keep the job indefinitely."

Chapter 7

Shut Down and Alone

If I could have allowed myself the privilege of emotion, I don't think I'd ever have stopped crying. I couldn't have real friends because I thought they could see what an awful person I knew I was, obviously that's why they didn't include me in their lives. I couldn't talk to anyone. Who would listen? Who could like me, a worthless, used, ugly worm? No wonder none of the lads in our youth club wanted to go out with me.

There was only one thing that I stood my ground on against my stepfather and that was going to the only place I could feel safe, a place where I felt loved and I where I found security – the local church.

When I went there I'd get a warm, tingly sort of feeling. I didn't understand it; it wasn't the group I was with because they were the same "friends" who never invited me to join them. I joined in with them at the various groups the church offered, but I never really felt one of them.

Something kept attracting me back again and, moreover, enabled me to stand up to the barrage of comments my stepfather made to me at home like, "You treat this place like a hotel on Sunday's" and, "Christians! Stab you in the back as soon as look at you." Or, "They're all two faced, back stabbing, double dealing…" He was always looking for opportunities to discredit anyone at the church and to humiliate me so that I wouldn't go back.

When I was old enough I went a Communion service at nine thirty in the morning followed by an eleven o'clock service where I taught the Sunday school children and then in the evening I went to CYFA (Church Youth Fellowship Association). Communion services were the ones that sent the "warm tingling feelings" through my body which I didn't understand at all.

My Vicar and CYFA leaders were fantastic. Whenever I went to CYFA I had to give three rings on the telephone to let my parents know that I had arrived there safely. One evening all I got was the engaged tone. I tried several times but each time it was still engaged. That familiar feeling churned my insides and I felt like a rabbit caught in the headlights of the car in the middle of a dark country lane. I knew that the failure to phone them would mean that I would be in so much trouble and I couldn't concentrate on what was going on in the group. After about twenty minutes or so I could cope no longer and burst into tears. The other teenagers were stunned and could not comprehend why I was so distraught, none of them had ever to ring their parents.

The group was run in the home of a young couple, Jill and Daniel. Jill told me she would sort it out for me. She rang the telephone company who determined that the telephone had been left off the hook and sent a tone down my parents' line. Jill then spoke to my stepfather who was very understanding, polite and thanked her for letting him know.

"It's a good job Jill rang when she did because I was just about to come round there and haul you out in front of your friends to give you a bloody good hiding for not ringing." My stepfather spat at me as I walked through the front door. I didn't argue or try to defend myself. What was the point? From that night Daniel picked me up and took me home each week.

Many times I play acted in my mind as I lay in bed. Always the same scenarios where I was ill in hospital, not with anything serious, but I had a long term illness. I would snuggle the duvet around me and pretend that the nurses were hugging me and that they loved me. Night after night I rehearsed telling either my Vicar or Jill and Daniel what was going on at home. I knew these conversations were never going to become a reality.

To the world, we were the ideal family; a man who had taken on some-one else's children and had provided for them. The perfect family was nothing more than an illusion, all the time behind closed doors I was living a life of hell.

I went to a local college to study the "Bi-lingual Secretary Course" and I managed to get myself a Saturday job in a department store. The guy who worked in the stock room wanted to go out with me. I was flattered and shocked. We had a works party and he offered to take me home, so I rang my stepfather. "Hi, it's me. You don't have to come and pick me up Jake; the guy I told you about will drop me home."

"No. I will come and pick you up. Be where I dropped you off by ten." His words were once again, that sharpened blade that sliced me in two.

I got in the car. "You are forbidden to see him, he is twenty-one and you are only seventeen, he lives in his own flat and drives a car. You are at college and boyfriends and study don't mix. There will be plenty of time for boyfriends when you are much older. Besides, of all the girls that work in that store, why on earth would he want to go out with you?" It was as if I could see the bullet racing toward me but could not move. It hit me square in the forehead. I knew that the real reason was because my stepfather just didn't want me to have a boyfriend so I decided to see Jake anyway. This defiance gave me a sense of control over my life.

Wrong decision! I went back to his flat, he gave me a guided tour then announced, "I don't expect us to go to bed together straight away; we can explore each other's bodies for a couple of weeks first!"

I knew that this relationship was wrong but because it gave me some power at home I didn't want to end it, even though it meant I spent the next six or seven months sneaking around and fighting Jake off my body.

One day the abuse ended on one of my stepfather's 'driving lessons', my stepfather had me park the car in a lonely, quiet place and by the time

I had stopped the car, his trousers were undone. He asked me, "Will you hold it for me?" My hands were like a vice on the steering wheel; this was the first time he'd ever asked me, ever given me a choice.

I looked ahead, "No." I replied emphatically.

"If you love someone enough you'll do anything for them." He pleaded.

"You are meant to be my father!" I hissed and my grip tightened on the steering wheel.

To my shock, he did his trousers up, muttered and mumbled, and snapped at me to drive home.

"Oh, you're back early!" Mum was watching television. She looked at us as if a question mark hovered over her head. "Is everything alright?" She enquired.

"Yes. I'm going to bed." I replied. "Goodnight Mum. See you in the morning." I didn't know what to think. This was the first time he had actually stopped when I said so. Was this the end? Or was this just another lull? Would he be up to say goodnight?

Even though nothing happened again, I lived in fear always waiting for the next time. On my wedding day, I made sure that I was not left alone in the house with my stepfather. My friends' husband was driving us to the church so I made sure that he arrived before Mum and my bridesmaids left, just in case my stepfather wanted one last go.

Chapter 8

Wrenched Apart

As the day wore on I realised that I was thirsty, so my nurse Chris, let me have sips of water. Once I had begun to drink without vomiting they removed my drip. I decided that I wanted to go to the toilet but was not allowed to get up from my bed, so three midwives tried to lift me on to a bed pan. I had forgotten what agony labour had been; now I felt physically sliced in two. I could not sit up so they tried to lift my bottom to lay me on it. It took ages and I was crying out in pain at the slightest movement. Eventually they got me on the pan and even though I had such a full bladder I couldn't do anything. One of the nurses had a good idea that the sound of running water might help so they turned the taps on. They could have brought Niagara Falls in and that wouldn't have helped either. So we had to reverse the process and get me off it. I didn't want to go through that again! Eventually later on, nature took its course and my bladder was relieved!

It was decided that my Mum could come to visit me in place of Donald that night, because he was still with Gabrielle in London. I remember Mum coming with my stepfather, but was so drowsy that I don't know what was said.

Chris, my nurse had been so kind to me and had been with me all the time I had been on the ward. Every time I had drifted into consciousness, she was there for me, to talk to and hold my hand. I really missed my nurse when she went off duty. Now I was totally alone and I found myself becoming anxious as the time wore on and Donald had not come back from London. Was he all right? What was happening to Gabrielle?

Eventually, around midnight, he came back. "Where have you been?" I snapped, "I've been wondering what's been going on."

"Oh don't – it's been a nightmare." Donald sighed. "After going up in the ambulance, I had to come home by train which only went part of the way. I had trouble finding a connecting train and in the end couldn't be bothered, so caught a cab for the rest of the journey. I didn't care about the cost – I just wanted to get back here."

As he sat there and held my hand he said, "Gabrielle has had one operation and is on various monitors and a ventilator. The surgeon had to go and perform another operation so didn't have much time to talk to me, I don't really know much. The nurses there are really nice and they gave me some more Polaroid photographs for you. I'll go back up there again tomorrow and see how things are doing."

His words lifted a load from my burdened body. Gabrielle wasn't dead and had survived an operation – I was so relieved.

"How are you, Jeany?" Donald turned his attention to me. Despite not having slept for the last twenty-four hours, all Donald was concerned about was how I felt. His tired, lovely blue eyes showed his love for me as he held my hand. My mind was a blur of anaesthetic, emotion and pain. I heard myself say, "Ok I suppose. I missed you and I miss Gabrielle. It's not fair. I'm tired but can't sleep. My tummy really hurts. I want you to stay with me. I want Gabrielle here. Oh, I don't know – it's all so complicated and confusing."

Donald tried to reassure me, "I know, but it will soon be all sorted. Try not to worry. I'm going home now to get some sleep. I have been given a free hand to visit both you and Gabrielle whenever I want to. I'll come in to see you in the morning before I go to London and then come back again later in the day to let you know how Gabrielle is doing." Donald leant over and kissed me. "Try to get some sleep. I love you."

"Love you too. See you tomorrow." Donald left and I lay there thinking about so many things that my mind was one big mush.

The next day I had to get out of bed and have a bath. It was agony – although not quite as bad as the previous day's attempt at the bedpan!

I was moved into a sideward with another lady, she, like everyone else, had a baby alongside her bed. I was desperate, in intense pain and very, very lonely. I could barely move but had to get myself fit enough to be able to manage without assistance if I wanted to go to London.

Visitors came, admired the photographs and tried to cheer me up. My Mum wanted one of the photographs to show people her grandchild. I really wanted all of them to myself; it was all I had of our daughter. I reluctantly gave her one and she promised to look after it. Why shouldn't she have one? I had six, but even so, with Gabrielle in London so far away these six photographs were all I had of my precious daughter with no guarantee I would ever see her again.

Even though we were in side rooms, there was a big table where everyone congregated for meals. When we were at the dinner table one day, all the mums were discussing how their babies cried a lot and one woman was upset because her baby was in the special care unit downstairs so she couldn't have him by her bedside. Naturally they asked me what I'd had. I told them a little girl, but that she was in a hospital in London because she was born with her gut outside her tummy. The woman, who had been upset about her baby being downstairs, changed her attitude and realised how lucky she was to be able to visit him whenever she wanted to.

Knowing how good breast milk is for babies, it was always my intention to breast feed Gabrielle. A midwife showed me how to express my milk, and then I did it every four hours to keep the supply going. I had to do it by hand to begin with then once the milk had come through I used a machine. It gave me something to do for Gabrielle and something to oc-cupy my time during all those lonely hours.

Every day Donald travelled between Gabrielle and me – I always knew when he was coming because I'd hear the midwives asking him how my little girl was doing on his way through to me. Donald's employers were very sympathetic to our plight and signed him off work for another week blaming the operation he had had on his knee, and then said they would sort out more time off for him after that if he needed it. No one knew how long this situation was going to last.

All I had ever wanted was a normal, happy birth of our first baby – to be a family, to be photographed together and be complete, but it was far from it.

Sleep was a stranger. The days and nights merged together in one period of longing for my daughter. I was given sleeping tablets. I hugged Gabrielle's photographs in bed with me – somehow it made me feel closer to her. I vaguely remember one night that a midwife came and took them away and put them on the side because the lady I was sharing a room with, had seen that they were getting bent.

I tried to be cheerful and not get upset but it was so very hard. I kept a diary. Here is the first of the extracts.

__30th September__ – These past two days have been hard but I have coped fairly well without Gabrielle. Donald goes to see her every day and gives me up-dates on her progress, but what I really want is to see her myself. I have expressed quite a lot of milk for her and the midwives are very pleased with the amount I have produced.

Today was the worst day. I saw more of Donald but I think that made things worse, even though I didn't want him to go. All I want is my baby. She's mine and I don't even know what she is really like. I've got my photographs but I want her. I know that I've got to be strong to go to her and I have tried so hard not to get upset, but I can't help it now. I want her. Everyone else has got their babies or they can go downstairs and see and touch them, but I can't do anything. I love her, she's mine and I want to be near her, touch her, and tell her I love her.

I didn't manage to produce much milk tonight, I think it's because I have been upset all afternoon and evening and very tearful.

I have had some sleeping tablets again tonight but they have not taken effect quite so quickly. I am feeling much better physically, but I am getting backache from the position when I am expressing milk, which in turn gives me problems standing and walking, but my stomach feels reasonably good. Obviously there is still some pain and I am restricted in my movements, but on the whole I think that I have made a quick recovery.

I am afraid, though, that if I am not careful a breakdown in my emotions could pull my physical state down. I was happier yesterday when I was told that I might be able to go to London at the weekend, but since then nothing more has been mentioned to me but a lot of other people have been told that they can go home soon because of a shortage of beds. I can't wait another six days without my darling baby. I want to go up there, as I was promised, stay there for a week or so, then I will be travelling to and fro, depending on how Gabrielle is doing and how much longer she is likely to be there. Donald and I can arrange living at home and visiting her in between Donald going to work. At least we will both see her every day.

I need her now. I can't bear to be without her any longer. She is a part of me that has been inside me for thirty-four weeks and now suddenly she is not there anymore and she is not even in my sight. I'll have to have a word with a doctor tomorrow and Donald can have a word in London, then they should be able to work it out between them.

The sleeping tablets seem to be taking effect now, as I am very drowsy. It's quarter past twelve. My legs are feeling much better since I have been lying on my bed with them up rather than sitting, the swelling has gone down a bit. All I want is my baby back.

Saturday 1ˢᵗ October *– I woke up a few times from about three-thirty. I went to the toilet and was still upset. I kept on dreaming about my darling baby. I don't know what but I know it was Gabrielle. Every time I think of her I get tearful.*

Daylight streamed through the windows but I didn't want to get up. I felt so tired and emotional. At breakfast time, I didn't know if I could trust myself to keep control with everyone around me talking about their babies. I ate my breakfast quickly so that I could get away to do my expressing. I left the table early and went back to express my milk, but when I walked into the room a midwife was just finishing making my room-mate's bed.

I was torn. As is usual for me I wanted to put on a brave face and not cry, but really I wanted someone to notice me and realise how upset and desperate I was to see my baby. I asked her, "Do you want to do mine now?"

I was astonished when she looked at me kindly and said, "What's up?"

The damn exploded and all my pent up emotions burst out. "I want my baby!" I sobbed. "I can't wait any longer and don't want her to die before I get to see her again. I only saw her for a minute. It's not fair! I want my baby."

She put her arm around me and gave me a cuddle and offered me lots of comforting, soothing words as we began to look at Gabrielle's photographs, "I'll have a word with the doctors to see when you can go to London." She was lovely and very understanding. "I've tried so hard not to get upset but I can't help it now, I just don't know what to do with myself and I don't want to cope anymore." I crumpled. She promised to have a word and see when I could go.

While we were looking at Gabrielle's photographs and another midwife came along and joined in. Then it came, the news that I could go to London tomorrow! My stitches were removed which hurt a little but one was particularly difficult to remove and that hurt a lot. I didn't care, I was going to be with my baby, I was floating on air.

I packed most of my things into the case for Donald to take home because I wouldn't need them I'd have to wear clothes in London so Donald would have to bring me some in. This news lifted the cloud of fear and despair that had been with me since Gabrielle's birth. My lighter mood was reflected by the fact my milk yield increased quite significantly.

My neighbour Faye, my Mum and Donald all came to visit. I was on a high waiting for the next day to arrive.

"Hello, Jeany." Donald greeted me with a kiss, "Gabrielle has had most of her pipes removed today and they are very pleased with her progress. I had a twenty minute cuddle with her today and the nurse took a photograph of us with our camera." His happiness was clearly evident – even before he said anything. I could hardly believe that within twenty-four hours I too would be holding my precious daughter in my arms for the very first time.

It seemed that the hands of the clock were made of lead and time passed so slowly. I wanted it to go quickly. Chris, the student nurse who had cared for me on Gabrielle's birth day, was once again on duty. She came round to have a chat and was really pleased that I was going to London. As Donald was leaving she came to say goodbye to him and wish him well. Later on she came round again to say goodbye to me and wished me all the best with Gabrielle. She is a really genuine caring person and she will never know the positive impact she had upon me in my hours of need.

I couldn't wait until the morning so I could go to see my darling baby, kiss her, cuddle her and just be her loving Mummy. I couldn't believe that I had so much love to give to her. I never knew a love like this existed.

Chapter 9

Together at Last!

The next day was Sunday and I felt so excited. I was told that the ambulance would be here sometime after ten o'clock that morning. With a feeling of anticipation and excitement, I telephoned Donald, "Donald, hurry up and get here so that you are ready when I am to go to London. I can't wait to get out of here and see Gabrielle."

Donald tried his best to calm me, "Ok. I'll be as quick as I can but I have things to do. Be patient – you'll get there."

I put the receiver down. His words had little effect on me. It was alright for him to talk about patience, he'd seen Gabrielle every day and I hadn't seen her since the day she was born!

Panic ensued when the ambulance crew arrived to take me at exactly ten o'clock. It seemed as though unseen forces were trying to prevent me from seeing my daughter but the midwives were on my side and made the doctor hurry up so that I could get going. The ambulance crew, Stephen and Bethany reassured me that they weren't going to leave me no matter how long they had to wait.

The journey to London seemed to take forever even though it was just over an hour. Donald took the opportunity to follow the ambulance in our car so that he could get to know a better route. We would get to know this journey very well in the coming weeks and months.

At last we arrived and then it was Donald's turn to lead the way to Gabrielle's ward! I had quite a long walk around the hospital, which was a bit of a struggle, but as I realised we were nearing the ward I began to get faster. Stephen carried all my expressed milk to be put in the freezer and Bethany had a little giggle at my "speed". We had spoken so much about

43

Gabrielle on that long journey to London that they insisted on taking me right on to the ward so that they could meet Gabrielle.

As soon as we got there, Helen, Gabrielle's nurse found me a chair, wrapped Gabrielle in a blanket and handed her to me. It was such a tremendous feeling to be able to hold my baby at last. I was so emotional and couldn't speak because I would only have cried.

I cuddled Gabrielle for quite a long time, but in the nicest possible way Helen turned to me and explained, "Mrs. Pavett. To give Gabrielle the best chance it is best that she stays under the Baby-therm as much as possible because she really needs to be under the ultra-violet lamp to help her jaundice. The more time she can spend under it now the less number of days she needs to be under it – if that makes sense."

I knew that it did but I didn't want to give up my baby. I had waited for this moment for so long. To hold Gabrielle helped to fill that ache in my heart I had been feeling.

"Why don't you go down to the canteen and get something to eat?" Helen asked kindly. "I'll give you some slips which will give you a meal each." She glanced at my face. "Don't worry, Gabrielle will be fine, you can have another cuddle later and I will show you how to do her four hourly care if you'd like me to, then you can do it yourself all the time you are here."

"Thank you, I'd like that." I replied submissively.

Donald and I went to get some dinner but I was in no mood to eat and just wanted to get back to the ward as soon as possible. I needed to do something more for Gabrielle so when I returned to the ward I expressed my milk again. Afterwards I had another precious cuddle with Gabrielle and then Helen, suggested that I ought to go and have a lay down to get some rest.

Helen and I became good friends. Weeks later she told me that she had taken one look at me that day and thought that I was about to collapse and she was very worried about me that is why she suggested I rest. I warmed to her and the care she expressed to me. Since the birth of Gabrielle the week had been the longest of my life, and good restful sleep was but a distant memory. The journey into London had aggravated the wounds that Gabrielle's birth had inflicted on my body. This woman was someone whom I could trust my daughter with and so for the first time I felt secure enough to sleep.

The room we were given was a typical motel style bedroom sparsely furnished but comfortable. It gave us an oasis of privacy. Not only did I have Gabrielle's birth wounds to contend with, but my breasts, in particularly the right one, were very sore and hard. I lay on the bed. Donald put hot flannels on my right breast, and so that I could get some sleep, Donald left to go and look around the shops. When Donald came back, I was still asleep, so this lovely man went and sat in the day room for a while. I woke up at five-thirty and at six o'clock went to find Donald so we could get some tea.

On returning to Gabrielle's ward, we had another cuddle. I cannot describe the love I feel for this baby – our creation. She was a part of both of us; I had nurtured her in my womb for thirty-four weeks and had been her lifeline. My womb had been barren, there had only been Donald and I, then by the miracle of creation, God had placed Donald's seed in the right place at the right time to fertilize my egg and create this beautiful daughter for us. It was beyond my comprehension. It had created a whole new meaning to life for me and stirred up emotions that were new to me.

I expressed some more milk before bedtime which had become my routine. My right breast had softened slightly but was still causing me

45

problems. Even though this was painful it was the one thing I could do for my daughter and so I would not give in and stop expressing my milk.

When we were alone getting ready for bed, I became overwhelmed with emotion. I cannot actually say specifically what it was. It was a whole mixture of my childhood experiences, fear for the future, the love for my daughter. I felt that I would burst and couldn't stop crying. Eventually exhaustion overcame us and we went to sleep.

The events of next day caused Donald and I to start to panic, I wrote this entry in my diary:

> *__Monday 3rd October__ – Gabrielle went into an incubator today. They said it was a step forward, which was a relief because Donald and I thought it was a step backwards. I couldn't wait for the ultra-violet lamp to be taken away because Gabrielle was so sore under her arms, neck, on her face and knees but nothing could be done about it until the photo-therapy was complete, plus she had to have a bandage over her eyes to prevent them from being damaged by the light. Those big, beautiful, blue eyes would look all around the room when we cuddled her. I wanted her to be able to see me all the time I was there, even in the incubator, to see how much love I had for her and to see her parents. Donald took quite a few photographs and a nurse took one of us as a family.*

The fact that Gabrielle only weighed four pounds seven ounces meant that I got depressed every time I thought that there was the possibility of her not being home for Christmas but despite my fears I loved to pass the time with Gabrielle by telling her what life would be like when we were all together as family at home. I couldn't bear it if anyone didn't agree with my optimism. All I had was hope and negative comments shattered my hopes and dreams. For example the head Sister was often talking about how babies didn't always survive these ordeals; she always seemed covered in a black cloud. Whenever she heard me tell Gabrielle to get better so she could come home for Christmas, she'd dampen my hopes by telling me that she had a long way to go. I nick-named her the "Doomy Gloomy Nurse".

The next day "Doomy Gloomy Nurse" came to us and announced, "I need you to vacate the room either tomorrow or the day after because a breast-feeding mum needs it."

I was horrified, "But my hospital only let me come because they thought I would have a room for the rest of my ten days confinement and it's not yet over." I countered. I felt as though my jaw was resting on the floor. I still had a couple of days to go and mentally I wasn't prepared to be turned out so soon. I couldn't bear the thought of leaving my baby behind again – I just didn't want to face it. I thought that she would be in hospital for a short time and that I would be able to stay there with her all the time.

"You have a long haul ahead of you my dear," the head sister told me, "and whenever there is a room available, you are welcome to stay, but we do need to give priority to parents whose babies are dying or preparing to go home." That was no consolation.

The day Donald took me home I felt as though a pack of hounds had caught me and I cried all the way home. Our conversation showed that we both felt exactly the same. From the back of the car I said, "I feel like I've left a part of me behind."

"You have." Donald remarked from the front of the car.

This baby had been inside me for so long, we were cruelly parted at her birth, reunited and now I was being sent away again. I didn't know what to do with myself. The journey was awful because of my operation anyway, let alone the added emotional pain I now felt.

We opened the front door; it didn't feel like a home anymore, we might as well have walked into the cells of an old castle, it was cold and dank and not the home I had left when pregnant.

I began to understand why the "Doomy Gloomy" Sister behaved the way she did and stopped calling her that name. Gabrielle was not expected to live. Donald hadn't told me before because I had been in a bad enough state being parted from her without the knowledge that they expected her to die. Only a short piece of gut had been trapped outside but the problem lay with the fact that the hole in her abdominal wall was only a small one and so the gut had got twisted. Part of it had been gangrenous, another part was damaged and moreover Gabrielle hadn't grown enough gut. Had she grown more gut she would have had a better chance, and if it had been the large intestine that had been trapped, it wouldn't have been as bad. Tragically it was her small intestine, which is the one that does all the work. The surgeon had left the damaged piece of gut inside and hoped that the rest would help it to recover. In the meantime Gabrielle had a colostomy and all we could do was wait, hope and pray.

I wanted to talk to God about all this but found it very hard to communicate with anyone. We loved Gabrielle with all our hearts and wanted to be a proper family. There are people all over the world who don't want children, but they continue to churn them out and they neither care about nor love them. I had so much love to pour out to this child and I might not get the chance.

Our vicar James, who was new to the parish and we'd not really got to know him very well, visited Gabrielle in hospital expecting me to be there and when I wasn't he came to see me at home. He kept in touch regularly and told us that people at church prayed for us even though some we barely knew.

Despite all the odds Gabrielle was a fighter and soon she no longer needed the phototherapy, heart monitor, oxygen saturation monitor or the incubator. She looked just like any healthy baby of her age and the only 'give-away' that there was something wrong, was the drip that fed her.

A month after she was born, Gabrielle went into a bassinette. It would have been sooner but they thought it was best that she stayed in the incubator until after the operation. Gabrielle's surgeon said that she had discovered good news and bad news. The outside layers of the poor gut had healed, but the inside layer hadn't and that was the important layer because that was the part that did all the work. The Consultant told us that she would leave Gabrielle for at least a month before she operated again. I still didn't give up hope that Gabrielle would be home in time for Christmas.

The next day Donald and I walked onto the ward and were shocked to find Gabrielle in a large cot with fans blowing on her. Overnight she had got an infection in her drip line which had caused a dangerously high temperature. This meant that they had to take her off the TPN (Total Parenteral Nutrition – the food drip) and she was on clear fluids through a temporary line. It was quite common for the babies to get infections in their drip lines when they had been in for some time, and a dose of antibiotics usually cleared it up quite quickly. Some babies get more infections than others and some are sicker than others but Gabrielle was only unwell for a couple of days then she soon bounced back and was back on the TPN again, with a new drip site.

The new central line was put in her head. I didn't like this idea at first, her hair had been shaved off to put the line in, but I found that it made dressing her easier and also we could actually bath her because the drip site wouldn't get wet being there.

As the weeks passed Gabrielle got stronger and better and just to give her a treat she was allowed a little glucose drink called dextrose. She drank it from a bottle and thoroughly enjoyed it. I was elated to give it to her.

Sometime later, Gabrielle got another infection in her line, it wasn't as bad as the first one and she recovered even quicker than before, but there was something that took much longer to heal and caused Gabrielle a lot of pain.

Chapter 10

"Leave Her Alone!"

One day I walked in to find an agency nurse attending to Gabrielle. She was a complete contrast to all the regular nurses. Every four hours the babies needed to have their nappies changed, mouths washed, eyes cleaned etc., and the regular staff always encouraged me to do as much of it I wanted to. This agency nurse did everything.

I went to pick Gabrielle up for a cuddle. "You sit in chair." She barked and pointed towards the chair. I robotically sat as I had been conditioned since childhood. It was as if she had a remote control pointed at me, my bottom jaw dropped to the floor. She handed Gabrielle to me. At first I wondered if it was because of the infection, but I soon realised that it was 'her way'. I didn't argue or challenge her, but inside I was screaming out, "How dare you treat me this way? I don't want to do what you're telling me, Gabrielle's mine. How dare you?"

Once again I was not in control of my own life or that of my child – and yet I did exactly as she commanded. I laid Gabrielle back in her cot on her side and went for a drink, but when I returned the nurse had placed Gabrielle on her tummy a position which she hated. I watched the nurse changing Gabrielle's nappy and couldn't believe what I was seeing. She had been using acid wipes to clean Gabrielle's tummy which had become red raw and Gabrielle was writhing about in agony, screaming uncontrollably and nothing would calm her down. I immediately went to the head Sister who was absolutely horrified.

I wanted to slap this nurse and tell her exactly what I thought of her, but I didn't. I was in tears, Gabrielle was in tears and Donald had to hold

Gabrielle down so that the Sister could remove the adhesive pad that kept the bag in place and put some ointment on her tummy to help the burn.

Afterwards I gave Gabrielle the dextrose to try to calm her down. I held Gabrielle close to my chest, my stomach in knots and I felt so much physical pain. I never wanted to stop cuddling her anyway – particularly when she was upset or hurt but at that time I wanted to cuddle her even more and make everything better in the security of my arms. Gabrielle was a very cuddly baby and always held on to me tightly whenever I held her. She was so warm and love radiated out from her.

Later, Gabrielle got really upset again when it came to cleaning up her tummy and she cried so much that three or four inches of gut came out. Donald rushed out of the room got Sarah, one of the nurses. Urgently he said, "Sarah, Jeany is changing Gabrielle's nappy and Gabrielle's screaming so much that her gut is coming out!"

"Don't panic, Donald," Sarah replied calmly, "it's nothing to worry about and often happens when a baby is in distress. We can usually push it back in. Do you want to hold Gabrielle Jeany while I try to push it back in again? I nodded but Gabrielle was screaming and I was crying so Sarah said that it wouldn't do any harm to leave it.

A new head Sister took over called Sylvia. I made sure that she knew that I didn't want that agency nurse to ever look after Gabrielle again and she respected my wishes.

My neighbour Faye wanted to see Gabrielle and so one day in November, I took her and Amy with me. When we got there Gabrielle had managed to pull her drip out. We spent a bit of time with her until a junior doctor came along to put a new one in. I wanted to hold her while he did it. The other doctors had always let me; it made a calmer baby when she was in my arms rather than being pinned down on a bed, but this doctor wouldn't hear of it. I was in the same room but not allowed anywhere near

Gabrielle. The doctor made such a meal of it that Gabrielle was screaming in agony, he was stabbing her all over and cursing because he couldn't get the needle in a vein. "I think it would be easier to do if you weren't in the room." He glared under his arm at me.

Faye guided me into the day room, across the corridor and closed the door behind us, the door of Gabrielle's room was also closed and yet we could still hear her screams of pain. I paced the floor, desperate to go back in to her. I was torn between pure fury and hatred which made me want to go and stab that doctor around with a needle to see how he liked it and pure love for my daughter. I was consumed with desperation to go to her and hug her better. The doctor still couldn't do it and ended up storming off in a temper.

Gabrielle's Consultant came and did it herself in the end with no trouble at all and she was not amused by this doctor's behaviour.

Chapter 11

Christmas in Hospital

Christmas was fast approaching and we knew that Gabrielle wouldn't be home. We had spent every day with Gabrielle since I was discharged from hospital; sometimes it was only for an hour or so but when possible it was several hours. If I drove up there myself while Donald was at work I could spend the whole day with Gabrielle rather than sitting there counting the minutes until Donald came home to take me. On these occasions I'd make him rush his food or we'd go immediately he came through the door and eat at the hospital. We had no life together. If I went to the hospital on my own during the day Donald and I at least had some time in the evenings together.

I devoted every second of my time in London to Gabrielle. I only left her side when it was absolutely necessary. We played, laughed, talked, cuddled – it was just so wonderful to be with her. She had all her own toys; clothes and equipment, except the cot, in her room and it became our own little home. The nurses kept out of the way as much as they could so we had as much privacy as a busy London hospital could afford. Whenever it was possible, we stayed in one of the rooms at the weekends so we could have lots of time with Gabrielle and time together without rushing to and fro. We had become very good friends with the nurses and they loved Gabrielle. Lots of babies came and went quickly but Gabrielle and another little one called Samantha were long-term.

Gabrielle was a very contented little girl. She would lie there watching her mobile going round and looking at her toys that crowded her cot. There was nothing I didn't love about this little daughter of ours. All I wanted was for her to be better and come home with us.

54

Just before Christmas, her Consultant took Gabrielle back to theatre and discovered that she had grown some more gut and so was able to join everything together and close up the stoma. We were so happy that everything seemed to be going right at last, and it seemed we were a step nearer to all going home. We were so excited when Gabrielle opened her bowels for the first time in the normal way!

We bought a small Christmas tree and some decorations and put them up in Gabrielle's room. I didn't feel like decorating our home because our Christmas would be in London, but despite this, I put a few up anyway.

I was devastated when my Mum and stepfather had decided that they were going to visit us in hospital on Christmas Day. My past fears came to haunt me. "I wanted the day to be for just Donald, Gabrielle and I!" I muttered, afraid to object too much, but my insides screamed out, "I don't want you here – stay away and stop trying to organise me!"

"We'll not stop long, we just want to come up and see her on Christmas morning." My stepfather replied.

I didn't have the strength to answer and Donald didn't really understand my logic, so I asked,

"What time are you planning on coming then?" hoping that they would respect my wishes and not come. Not a chance! They had also already arranged to bring Donald's Mum and Dad with them.

"We're not sure yet, but we won't stop long." My stepfather continued.

Christmas morning arrived and Donald and I woke in our own home, had some breakfast and opened a couple of presents before making our way to our beloved daughter. Being Christmas morning the roads were quieter, and the journey seemed much shorter. My elation at getting to the hospital quickly was cut short.

As we entered the ward we were greeted by my stepfather pacing the floor. "Where have you been? We've been here ages." He snapped in a tone and manner which was typical of the way he addressed me throughout my childhood and I crumpled inside, reprimanded. The brief tension between us was broken.

"You've missed Father Christmas," my Mum said kindly, "I've taken a couple of pictures for you – it was really lovely. The nurses took a Polaroid photograph for you as well. One of the doctors was Father Christmas and went round to all the babies, gave them a present, but gave Gabrielle and Sammy a pillowcase full!" She was excited, obviously really happy to have seen it and wanted to share it with me because I had missed it. My love for my Mum began to melt my heart but all my mind could think of was that my stepfather had once again made decisions about my life.

I didn't care that he was annoyed because I didn't invite them there in the first place, but he had still made the decision. What he wanted he always got; he was a very forceful person. Not only did they know that we didn't want them there, but my Mum and stepfather had left my younger brothers and sisters at home – the youngest only being thirteen – with strict instructions that they were not to open any presents until they got back. If the tables were turned and my grandparents had tried to dictate to him, he would soon have put them in their place.

Anyway, after what seemed like hours, but was in fact only about twenty minutes, they went and we could then get on with our Christmas. We opened our stocking presents first of all, and then worked our way through Gabrielle's presents. She had so many. Unfortunately, because she was so young, she wasn't very interested, but I put a Christmas hat on her anyway and spent another day loving her.

Chapter 12

Up's and Down's

It was sometime around this Christmas that Gabrielle's Consultant told me that Gabrielle wouldn't be able to drink my milk so I stopped expressing it. She said that she hadn't realised I was doing it otherwise she would have told me sooner. Gabrielle would drink progestermil milk. I was disappointed because I had really wanted to be able to breast feed her.

In January Gabrielle's Consultant decided that Gabrielle's gut had healed enough to start trying Gabrielle on the milk, which would be fed through a Nasogastric tube. I was also able to feed her some baby rice, progressing to liquidized vegetables to be introduced one by one in case there was a reaction to any one of them. It seemed a real step in the right direction, a giant leap forward. We were so excited!

One Saturday in January became a special day for us. Our Vicar, James, with one of the churchwardens, as a representative of the church, came to baptise Gabrielle in the hospital. Only our immediate families and Gabrielle's Godparents were there. Gabrielle was wide awake during the preparations, but sound asleep during the ceremony and social bit afterwards. Once everyone had gone home, she woke up again! We were able to use a camcorder to capture this momentous day – everything seemed so "normal".

That evening Donald and I went out for a social night with the nurses and the parents of the other poorly baby, Samantha. It was a good night out, a great meal and lots to drink. We really enjoyed the whole day and evening.

Now back to my diary:

> *24th January – It is a long time since I wrote anything*
> *down, but so much has happened. Despite all the odds, our*
> *"little fighter" lives on. Gabrielle is being fed on three-quar-*
> *ter strength progestermil milk through a Nasogastric tube. It*
> *has gone up from quarter strength at one millilitre per hour*
> *to three-quarter strength at fourteen millilitres per hour. The*
> *amount is raised by one millilitre every day at twelve o'clock in*
> *the afternoon. She seems to be taking it well and is, therefore,*
> *having her drip turned down. Hooray!!*

Life with Gabrielle was one of seemingly endless ups and downs. The 'up' of her rapidly improving feeding was countered by a 'down' of a cold. For many, this would be a minor ailment, but even a small sniffle rang loud warning bells in my head. Gabrielle had a cold, which even after a fortnight she had not been able to shake off. In fact, it seemed to be getting worse to me. When they gave her the routine injections that every baby has, I was beside myself with worry. I had heard so many scary stories about babies having bad reactions, especially to the whooping cough vaccine. I attempted to mention it to Alison the Sister, but she started saying, "Statistically..." I stopped her in her tracks.

"Statistically I should never have had a baby with Gabrielle's condition..." I interrupted, "one in thirty thousand babies are born with this condition and two out of three are sorted out straight away and that leaves only one in three in our position. To my mind, that gives us a 'one in ninety-thousand' baby!"

"Point taken," Alison said, "but honestly, Gabrielle's better off with the injections." Once again I had to shut my mind to what was happening as the familiar twin feelings of helplessness and powerlessness, suffocated me.

I want Gabrielle home with me – especially as she wasn't well. I discovered that her nappy hadn't been changed since about one o'clock in the afternoon and we arrived at six-thirty in the evening. I wished that she was nearer to home so that I could spend more time with her, and give her the care she deserved.

Another fear arose in my mind; my relationship with Donald. Since Gabrielle's birth, we haven't had time to talk much or listen to music together like we used to; or anything else for that matter. Despite knowing this, I am not in the right frame of mind for any kind of relationship with him because I am exhausted, upset and frightened of what might happen with Gabrielle. How long can we cope? Our lives now revolve around travelling to and from London to be with her, and apart from the emotional strain, it is costing us a fortune! I feel that all this is my fault. I'll carry on though and do what I usually do, suppress my emotions and put a brave front on. No one, not even Donald, will ever begin to understand my feelings.

It was during February that I had the growing thought that Gabrielle is really unwell. One night one of the nurses rang us at home and said that Gabrielle had a temperature, they had telephoned Gabrielle's Consultant who had said that her feeds had to be stopped. When I got to the hospital at seven thirty-five the next morning, I could see that Gabrielle was shattered. She had been awake most of the night. They had removed her drip, taken blood for cultures. There was a problem accessing her veins and because the on-call staff could not get another line in, the Consultant had to come in and do it. The severity of the situation was highlighted in the fact that it had even taken her two hours to successfully complete this simple procedure.

This trauma caused Gabrielle to sleep quite a bit, but she was restless and cried in her sleep. I stayed until mid afternoon. Eventually, Helen took Gabrielle from me so that I could reluctantly go home. Gabrielle didn't want to be laid in her cot she only wanted to be cuddled. It broke my heart to leave her and the journey, as well as the time until I could return, was filled with anxiety and a longing to be with her again.

As soon as Gabrielle's feeds stopped, she went back to sucking a dummy. It was obviously a comfort thing because all the time she had something to eat or drink, she wasn't at all interested in it.

It has often been said that the bond between a mother and her baby is strong. The bond between Gabrielle and me even had another dimension to it. I had been told on many occasions that Gabrielle cried a lot at night, so whenever I stayed at the hospital I told the nurse caring for her to wake me up when Gabrielle cried. Not once did she cry during the night while I was there!

I didn't sleep properly waiting for the knock at the door and used to go in to see her anyway.

Secretly, I wanted her to wake during the night so I could have some extra cuddles, but she didn't. One night I had to smile at her; the nurses had taken her nappy off because she had a sore bottom and they wanted to let the air get to her skin to help it to dry up. She was laid on the nappy and a clear plastic tunnel was placed over her bottom half to prevent her from rolling around and soiling the bed. When I went in to see her, she had wriggled down the bed and was right inside the tunnel with her hands clasped around her head. She looked so cute and cosy. I wished I had taken a photograph of her.

Sister Esther, a nun from the Priory which was local to the hospital regularly came in to see the children and talk with any parents who wanted someone to talk to. She was a really lovely lady who cared deeply about all the children and parents in the hospital. I had quite a few talks with her and enjoyed her company. We talked about my hopes for the future, how I couldn't wait to take Gabrielle home and begin our life as a family.

Due to all the problems Gabrielle had with her drip, her Consultant decided that it would be a good idea for her to have a Broviac line fitted. Basically, this was a more permanent drip line that went into the chest and it also meant that we would be able to change the drip ourselves and remove it completely for part of the day. We had to wait for a slot to come up on the operating list. I was really excited about this because it could also mean that we would be able to have trips out of the hospital without having to worry about the drip. There was even the possibility of a trip home for a few hours. It was a wonderful piece of news and I couldn't wait for the Consultant to take Gabrielle to theatre and fit it.

Chapter 13

Over-Ruled Again

The telephone rang suddenly and when I answered it was my Mum. She told me that as my stepfather was working in London he could take my Mum and me to the hospital for the day and then bring us home again later. I was reluctant to do this because that meant I wouldn't get any time alone with Gabrielle. For my Mum's sake I am glad that I agreed as she and I had a really special time together and with Gabrielle.

Cheryl, a lovely nurse from Scotland, suddenly came into the room. In a warm Scottish lilt she told us that there was a space in theatre so Gabrielle could go and have a Broviac line fitted. She said she would give me warning when they were ready to take her down. In the meantime I undressed Gabrielle, dressed her in a theatre gown and waited. There was never a time when Gabrielle had to have a procedure or operation when I wasn't scared or apprehensive but this procedure was going to give us all more freedom. I was also relieved at the thought that this operation would allow Gabrielle more comfort and so my normal apprehension was tempered by these thoughts.

While Gabrielle was in theatre, my stepfather returned from work. "Are you ready then?" he snapped. As usual he was only thinking of himself and whilst the offer to take my Mum and I to spend the day with Gabrielle seemed generous it was, always, on his terms.

"Gabrielle has just gone down to theatre to have a drip fitted, love," my Mum explained, "and Jeany wants to wait for her to come back before we go." I could see my stepfather's mood changing and the last thing I wanted was a scene of any sorts. The only thought in my head was to remove him out of the hospital.

"It's okay for you to go, Mum. I really don't mind. Donald will come and pick me up later in the evening." I spoke pleadingly.

"We might as well wait." My stepfather paced the floor impatiently, and looked at his watch.

His tension was filling the room and I needed to get out of the room so I made some sort of excuse and escaped to the day room where I knew there was a telephone. I rang Donald and told him what was happening and he was quite prepared to come and get me later on, after all we had planned to come for the evening anyway.

On returning to Gabrielle's room I announced, "I've just talked to Donald and he wants to come and see Gabrielle so you are free to go whenever you like."

I longed to see my stepfather leave. By now he was in a belligerent mood and even though earlier he couldn't wait to go, he now insisted that he would wait for me.

"Donald's been at work all day; you don't want to drag him all the way up here when we are here already. How much longer will she be?" My stepfather insisted.

I wanted to scream out "Just go and leave me alone. Donald will come and get me!" My heart and soul were breaking once again like so many times before, my stepfather was in control – telling me how I had to live my life.

Gabrielle took ages to come back to the ward and my stepfather was still pacing up and down in the corridor. I felt uncomfortable and wished that he would just go home and leave me there. When Gabrielle eventually came back, I took her from the nurse and gave her a cuddle. She was groggy and crying. I sat down with her in the chair and felt her pain. I was also very much aware that my stepfather was now ready for us to leave. I didn't want to leave my beloved child and desperately wanted them to go and for Donald to come to us. Even though it was only a little operation, Gabrielle was still upset and crying.

"You've seen her and she's alright," he said impatiently, "we've got to get back now as we're going to hit all the traffic at this time. Come on!" I felt that I had to hand my baby over to the nurse because he was ready to go. As usual it was all about him without a thought to my feelings as it was quite clear to everyone that what Gabrielle needed right now was to settle and to fall asleep in her Mummy's arms.

It was torture for me to let my baby go. I wanted to be there and cry with her, comfort her and make her feel better and loved. Apart from the first operation when I was in hospital myself, I had been there for Gabrielle, every time she had come back from her other operations to hold and soothe her.

When two of my sisters had their tonsils out as little children, my parents had spent every possible minute with them and he should have respected my wish to be with my child now. The age of the child makes no difference to the pain you feel as a mother when your child is suffering. It is often the hours after an operation where complications can set in.

For as long as I live I will never forget what we went through with our little girl, the pain is deep and the scars raw, but I will also never forget the added pain caused to me this day. Why couldn't my Mum stand up for me? Surely she understood how I was feeling? She never had in the past so why should I expect anything different now, but I did? I sat in the back of the car silently staring out of the window, fighting back my tears.

Once home, I telephoned the hospital many times to check that Gabrielle had settled down. She had calmed down but that didn't take away the emptiness, hurt and the feeling that I had let her down, betrayed her, and left her when she really needed me.

As I feared Gabrielle swelled up after the operation and became snuffli-er; they said it was a reaction to the anaesthetic. Gabrielle began projectile vomiting and so her Consultant ordered a contrast study to be carried out. Her feeds were stopped. I had really been enjoying liquidizing vegetables, chicken and fish for her and best of all feeding her. This routine was as close to normality for which I craved. I consoled myself because this contrast study would give a good picture of her gut to see exactly what was causing the problem.

We were really enjoying the freedom of not having the drip attached. Extra TPN was put through when we were not at the hospital so that we could have a few hours of freedom and walk around the whole ward. Don-ald and I were looking forward to being able to take her out in the pram and we had planned outings in the London parks and showing Gabrielle the sites.

I was getting very proficient at Gabrielle's medical care and one day Cheryl taught me to change the drip myself, so that I would be able to do it if I wanted to – anything I could do for Gabrielle I wanted to do!

Unfortunately tests showed that Gabrielle had developed bronchilitis and RSV (Respiratory Syncytial Virus – a highly contagious virus and can cause very serious illness in some children) so we had to keep her in the room so that the other babies didn't catch it. It was obviously very disap-pointing that we were restricted to the room, but we still had more free-dom without the drip always being attached.

The day came for the Contrast Study. Gabrielle enjoyed her barium meal! She drank it readily, which was not surprising as she was very hun-gry. They took quite a few x-rays throughout the day as they watched the meal pass through her system.

During the week that elapsed between the two studies of Gabrielle's stomach and intestines, she showed signs of normal childhood development. She learnt to push her toy wheel with the bell in it and seemed proud of her achievement; however, she was very frustrated at her inability to crawl. She knew what to do and had all the actions but she couldn't get herself to move. What Gabrielle didn't know was that the highly polished hospital floor gave her nothing to grip on.

This episode really showed her determination and her inquisitive nature, she wanted to explore her world and was not going to stop until she had done so. The experts say that when a baby is born prematurely its' development is expected to be slower than the average child. This was not the case with Gabrielle. She was only five months old and yet she was already trying to sit up by herself.

She also liked to sit on my lap and turned the pages in her little board books herself. She looked at the pictures as I 'read' them to her many times. She never seemed to tire of them.

The day for Gabrielle to have the contrast study to get a better look at her gut arrived. A dye was injected into her bottom so that they could track the journey as it travelled on an x-ray. I was with her the whole time during the study but Gabrielle hated it. She screamed the place down. Afterwards I carried her back up to the ward and gave her lots of cuddles and a nice bath. She didn't take long to settle down. It wasn't so much a painful experience for her but she was held down in the positions that the medical staff wanted which she didn't like. She knew her own mind.

They discovered that there was a section of gut that had narrowed which had caused the section before it to become swollen. Gabrielle needed more surgery to correct this. Gabrielle's Consultant thought it best to get this next operation over with before we went out with her, it was very disappointing news but it made sense.

Like all parents we wanted a record of Gabrielle's early life and although I took photos every day we decided to record her chattering away while she lay on her changing mat. However, recent events taught her how to scream and Gabrielle thought it was really clever.

Chapter 14

A Special Time

My first Mothering Sunday came and Gabrielle gave me a card and a box of chocolates. It was a lovely day. We took some beautiful photographs; it was a really special and lovely day for both Donald and me.

Whilst waiting for the operation, Gabrielle continued to develop. She now weighed in at seventeen pounds, seven ounces and measured twenty-six inches from the top of her head to her heel. A combination of being drip fed and beginning to cut her teeth caused her to bite anything that was hard. It appeared to be that she was constantly hungry.

The regime with her Broviac Line meant that now Gabrielle was free from it for about four hours a day (this means, disconnected from the drip). The aim was just to feed her while she was asleep.

It was the eve of Gabrielle's operation. Donald went home so that he was there for early shift in the morning and said he'd come back when he had finished work. During the course of the evening Sister Esther came round while I was playing with Gabrielle in her room and we began to talk. "Gabrielle's having an operation tomorrow so I'm staying here tonight. I love staying here and being so close to her. Would you like to cuddle her?" I said quietly.

"I would love to," replied Sister Esther. Her smile lit up her face and by the way she reacted thought suddenly occurred to me.

"Have you held Gabrielle before?" I asked.

"No. I don't pick the babies up when I visit." I was surprised at her answer.

"Oh I didn't realise that in all these months of you visiting Gabrielle, you have never held her." I handed Gabrielle to Sister Esther.

As she took Gabrielle into her arms she said very quietly, "Thank you so much. Gabrielle is very special." From the moment I had met Sister Esther I knew she was a person I could trust.

"Well you can hold her any time you want to – even if I am not here. I don't mind. Had I realised you didn't cuddle the babies I'd have said that earlier." I assured her.

After Sister Esther had gone I cuddled Gabrielle until she went to sleep. She took a long time to go off. As soon as she was asleep, safely in her cot, I quietly went to my room to grab some sleep. The first thing on my mind when I awoke was Gabrielle's operation and even though it was early, I went over to her room to reassure myself that she was alright.

As I entered I saw her nurse, Vicky who told me that Gabrielle had split her Broviac line during the night. In a way I was quite pleased because that meant I had complete freedom to have Gabrielle in my room for most of the day. We lay on the bed together cuddling and I watched the television. We played together, shared so much love and precious time. It was the most private we had ever been. Shut in my room, off the ward, no one could see or hear us. It was the closest we had ever been to being at home.

As I gave Gabrielle a bath something, she always loved, I remembered the time she threw herself backwards and had soaked the dressing on her drip line. When one of the nurses came to re-dress it, Gabrielle 'helped' by ripping the plaster off herself and I just managed to grab it before she pulled the whole line out. I made sure that today she once again had her set of ducks that she loved playing with in the bath. They were a mummy and three babies which sat on her back.

Every now and then a nurse knocked on the door and I had to take Gabrielle out to the ward so that a doctor could examine her in preparation for her operation, but then we went back into my room for more 'mummy and daughter' snuggles. I had so much love to give to my beloved daughter and it never seemed to end.

Eventually they came to mend her line and were almost ready for theatre. I dressed Gabrielle in her gown and continued to cuddle her while we waited for the call to go. I never stopped telling her how much I loved her. "Now then Gabrielle," I stroked her cheeks, "this time I want it to be your last trip to theatre so that we can all go home and start to live our lives together – for always – as a family should be. Okay darling?" Gabrielle looked at me, her beautiful face alight – all smiles. "Don't forget how much I love you. Daddy does too, and when you get back from theatre, he should be here with me. We both love you so much, Angel, and can't wait for you to get better so we can all go home. You are so beautiful, Mummy's Angel."

The telephone rang and it was time for Gabrielle to go. I went down with her, holding her hand all the way. When we arrived at the operating theatre I put my face next to hers and whispered,

"Don't forget Mummy loves you. Sweet dreams my precious little Angel." Gabrielle had her eyes fixed on me the whole time. "I love you so much, don't forget it. I love you darling. See you soon." I kissed Gabrielle, stroking her with my free hand. The bed began to push the theatre doors open and I had come to the end of my journey. My arm became more and more outstretched as the bed moved away from me through the theatre doors. At the last possible moment I let go and as the doors closed, Gabrielle was looking up over her head at me.

"I love you," I choked fighting back the tears as I walked back up to the ward and began the agonizing wait for Donald and Gabrielle.

Back in my room the emptiness engulfed me. I didn't know what to do with myself. The seconds became hours and the hours felt like days. I chatted to the nurses and spent some time watching the television to try to pass the time away. Donald arrived and was surprised that Gabrielle wasn't back. I remarked that they seemed to be taking so much longer this time. After what seemed like an eternity the theatre rang and said that the operation was over and Gabrielle was ready to come back on to the ward. One of the Ward Sisters, Alison, said that I could go down with her if I wanted, I didn't need a second telling – I was there.

The second I saw Gabrielle my "Mothers instinct" told me that something was terribly wrong. I managed to hold back the tears as I gave voice to my feelings. I said to Alison, "Something's wrong!"

Alison smiled kindly said reassuringly, "She has just had an operation.

"I know," I replied, still fighting the tears, "She has had four other operations and this time I <u>know</u> that something is wrong." My words were prompted from a feeling deep inside me and not from the state of the bed. As we headed toward the lift, it became apparent that Alison was not happy with the state of Gabrielle's bed. She was aware of my concerns and the amount of blood was clearly not helping. As she tried to wipe it up I remember her saying, "They could have cleaned this up a bit better, there's a lot of blood everywhere!"

I took Gabrielle's hand as we went back up to the ward. She squeezed my finger and opened her eyes looking straight at me, "Hello, Angel, Mummy's here and Daddy is waiting for us upstairs. I love you." I reassured her. Gabrielle closed her eyes and dozed off again. I didn't let go of her hand, "Mummy's here, Angel. I love you. I love you so much. I love you more than you will ever know."

Once back on the ward an oxygen box was put over Gabrielle's head with thirty percent oxygen being administered to her, but Gabrielle tried to push it away. She tried to cry and open her eyes but it was too much of a struggle for her. I stayed by her bedside until well into the night. Donald stayed there for a long time but he was tired from being on an early shift and then driving all the way to London afterwards.

Gabrielle's Consultant came to see us, "There were a lot of adhesions to be cut away and as a result Gabrielle suffered tremendous blood loss, she lost the equivalent of about two and a half volumes of blood – as fast as we were pumping it in it was coming straight back out like a waterfall. We have done what we needed to and now we just have to wait and see, but Gabrielle is very poorly," she explained.

Once again, we felt as though we'd been in a head on collision with a ten ton truck. We sat by Gabrielle's bedside in stunned silence. Later on that night I reluctantly went to bed but couldn't sleep properly. Something was very wrong. I could sense it, so I went back out to see Gabrielle. There were quite a few people around her bedside. She had been bleeding constantly and it wasn't clotting. It was then that I learned that Gabrielle had never had the normal number of platelets – which help the clotting process – until now it had not been a problem. The doctor on duty warned me that she might have to go back to theatre to have a blood vessel tied. He got me to sign a consent form just in case. I hated doing that. Donald had signed four and I had signed this last one and now was being asked to sign another.

Gabrielle's Consultant was called in at about five o'clock and said that she didn't think theatre was necessary as it was 'general ooze'. She instructed the nursing staff to apply pressure bandages and weigh them every time they were removed so that the blood loss could be calculated. Meanwhile more blood, platelets and plasma were being administered to her and I was getting more and more afraid. To my relief I felt Donald's reassuring presence at my side. He too had found sleep difficult and had come to join me in Gabrielle's room. Eventually we went back to bed but as I dropped off to sleep I dreamt horrible dreams and couldn't settle so got up again and went to hold Gabrielle's hand.

There wasn't a lot of difference from during the night. Gabrielle was given blood, plasma and platelets and regularly had blood taken from her for testing. It seemed that she wasn't making any platelets so couldn't clot very well. Everything began to go wrong; her blood chemistry was all over the place, for example, she was too low on calcium and too high on potassium, so constantly had to have different drugs to correct these levels, but as one level was corrected another went wrong. Thankfully the bleeding from her wound began to slow down. The doctors and nurses kept us informed throughout and never seemed to tire of my constant barrage of questions.

That evening Donald left for home because he had to go to work for an early shift the next day. I telephoned him at about two hours later to make sure that he had got home all right. He told me that he was going to go to bed to get some sleep and I returned to Gabrielle's side. I didn't leave her for any longer than I had to, even though the staff told me that I ought to rest. They assured me that they would come and get me if there was any change, but they might as well have talked to the brick wall. I couldn't rest or leave her side. Samantha's Mum offered to sit with Gabrielle while I rested but I didn't want to leave her.

The nightshift came on at nine o'clock and they were in for a night of it! They were short staffed so each member of the team had more work to do. The machine that was supposed to push the platelets into Gabrielle's drip line stopped working so Sue, the nurse looking after her, had to manually operate the pump. Someone asked her a question so she turned to face them. While she was turned, Gabrielle began to make some jerky movements. "Sue, Sue look at Gabrielle. What's happening?" I called, petrified. Sue turned to look at Gabrielle and called the doctor over. It was fit activity and the doctor gave Gabrielle something to calm her. It was fit activity which they couldn't be sure if it was due to the calcium deficiency or if the blood loss had affected her brain, anyhow the injection did calm her but I was really very frightened so I went to ring Donald and tell him to come back.

It was about eleven o'clock and the sound of the telephone roused Donald from his sleep. When he answered he thought it must be morning and that he had overslept. Eventually he focussed enough to realise it was me. I told him what had happened so he jumped in the car immediately and sped to get to us in record time. I went back to be by Gabrielle's side. Sue smiled kindly at me, "Are you alright, Jeany?"

I swallowed hard, "Donald's on his way back."

I watched while Sue continued to pump the platelets into Gabrielle.

"Sue! She's doing it again!" I screamed! This time it was different as I watched my beloved child, she stopped breathing before my very eyes.

The crash team were called in and I left the room, frightened, stunned and numb. While everyone rushed to Gabrielle one of the other parents made me a drink, then a nurse came and sat with me. She asked me if I prayed. Normally I did but I couldn't even do that. All I could think of was that Donald would get here and his daughter would already be dead. I remember wanting to go to the toilet but I didn't want to use the toilet on our floor because I would have had to pass Gabrielle so the nurse took me to another floor, then we waited in the nurses room. It was a horrible experience that I will never forget as long as I live, my darling, brave little girl was violently dying before my eyes and Donald seeming to take forever to get there. I felt so alone.

Then at last, the anaesthetist came up and sat with me, "We've put Gabrielle on a ventilator to help her breathe. She's had a respiratory arrest but not a cardiac arrest, all the fluid retention caused too much pressure on her lungs and made breathing too difficult for her. The ventilator will help her now." He tried to reassure me.

"She's not dead then?" I remarked relieved to hear his words. My tone surprised me as I sounded very matter of fact.

"No, certainly not, Gabrielle has been given drugs to keep her heavily sedated so she can't fight against the ventilator and try to breathe for herself. We've just got a couple more things to do then you can go back in and see her." He smiled kindly as he left.

Just then Donald arrived and I fell into his arms and tried to tell him what I had just been told but it was all so hard. We sat in our room while the team finished working on Gabrielle and Sue kept coming in to give us up-dates on the situation, but it seemed an eternity before we could see Gabrielle. Eventually we got to see her. I peered around the corner afraid of what I would find. Gabrielle lay on the bed with a tube down her throat breathing for her. Unlike Donald, it was the first time I had seen Gabrielle ventilated and the shock rooted me to the spot. Eventually we went to bed which seemed pointless. Quite apart from it being nearly morning, I could not sleep anyway.

Donald rang work just after six and they told him to take as much time off as he needed. It was another day and yet it seemed like the same day. I had lost all my senses, all I thought of was my child; I couldn't bear the thought of losing her. It had always been there in the back of my mind, but as time had gone by things had looked more positive so I tried to be; but now it was even harder to look on the bright side. Our vicar, James, had told me that someone in our church had a picture of a flower that kept opening and closing, they believed this to be Gabrielle. James said that he hoped that it would keep on opening. It didn't look very likely to me now.

We continued to encourage Gabrielle to pull through, told her we loved her and wanted her to come home.

Gabrielle retained more and more fluid. They had so much going into her, blood, drugs, fluids, and her body was retaining it all, her kidneys had stopped working and her liver wasn't doing its job properly either. Gabrielle's Consultant came to talk to us, "The situation is very grave. We are doing all that we can and we will continue to do so, but this is a battle we might not win. All we can do is hope and pray – the next twenty-four to forty-eight hours are critical."

We went back to our room and we both cried. We were helpless.

Donald telephoned our next door neighbour Faye and told her the situation; she rang round our families, Gabrielle's Godparents and James. The next thing we knew, James appeared. He had jumped in his car as soon as he had put the telephone down and driven to see us. Once he had all the details he rang his wife and got the church members praying for us. He was just about to go on holiday but told us that his curate would be there and if we did lose Gabrielle, to make whatever arrangements we wanted and it would be done.

We spent a long time with Gabrielle then went into the day room to pray, Samantha's Dad was there and he joined in. We also prayed for Samantha. James left and the hours ticked on by slowly. Sometime I went to bed.

Chapter 15

The Last Days

I awoke with a start, I had dreamt that they had switched Gabrielle's ventilator off. I stumbled onto the ward knocking into the walls and doors. Sue and Eileen wondered what was happening so in my panic I told them, "I just dreamt that you were switching Gabrielle's ventilator off so I had to come and see for myself that she is still alive."

"Jeany," Sue put her arm round me, "nothing like that will ever happen. Honestly. And if Gabrielle became worse, we would come to your room to talk to you."

I had to make sure that Gabrielle was all right, for myself. "Mummy's here. I love you, my little Angel." I stroked Gabrielle's forehead, kissed her and stumbled back to bed.

I wouldn't speak to anyone outside the hospital. I couldn't. Donald had to do all that. Faye was wonderful. She had been doing most of our washing and ironing and now she was doing the awful task of keeping everyone informed of this situation for us. I constantly felt as though I was going to be sick. I had never felt like this before, it was as though it was the whole of my insides that I wanted to bring up, my whole body heaved constantly. I was helpless. I could see our cherished daughter, lying there, drugged, ventilated and not responding to the treatment. Yes, there were little improvements now and again, but for every little improvement there was an even bigger setback.

I cannot stress how good the staff were. They tried to encourage me to get some sleep, but I didn't do much of that. I stayed by Gabrielle's bed side night and day, holding her hand and willing her to live. She had gained about five pounds in fluid retention making her face and eyes so swollen that she couldn't have opened them if she'd tried. Her body was stiff and she couldn't move. She was so bloated in addition to all the drugs that were rendering her unconscious. It was such an awful sight and there are no words that can truly describe my feelings. I so wanted to see an improvement, but there was none. I'd have done anything, chopped off my arm if necessary, and sacrificed my own life just to have my little girl out of that terrible situation.

Things went from bad to worse. Because of all the fluid retention the ventilator had to be on maximum strength, even so her oxygen saturation level still did not improve. It is supposed to be around a hundred – at least the late nineties – but Gabrielle's was in the eighties and lower. All this was a strain on every part of her body especially her heart. Because there had been some fit activity, they could not rule out brain damage until she came round from everything else.

They tried physiotherapy on her lungs but it didn't seem to be doing any good either. The days continued to roll into one. Donald went home to get some more clothes so I was alone when the Consultant came to Gabrielle's bed-side. She placed her hand on my shoulder and said, "Hang on in there! We're carrying on the fight."

There was one thing different about this day, Samantha's parents and the nurses persuaded us to go out for a drink during the evening. I didn't want to leave Gabrielle's side let alone the hospital and worried that something would happen while I was gone. The nurses told me that nothing would, and ordered me to go. They knew exactly where I was if necessary and it was only a minute from the hospital. I reluctantly agreed and made sure that I told Gabrielle that I was popping out and that I loved her before I left. We were out for a couple of hours and I had three drinks. On our return I spent more time with Gabrielle before going to bed where I think I had a record five hours sleep.

We entered a period of stalemate where nothing really seemed to be happening. Gabrielle wasn't improving, nor was she getting any worse and yet my senses told me that something was dreadfully wrong. I didn't want to hear any negative news so I avoided the Consultant by hiding in the bedroom leaving Donald by Gabrielle's bedside. There was a knock at the door and Helen came in for a chat. "How are you doing, Jeany?" she asked kindly. "The Consultant has been round to see Gabrielle and Donald, but she will come back again later when you are both around."

Pain seared through my body and I wanted to scream. Instead I calmly asked, "Why?" I was terrified that I already knew the answer.

"I don't know." Helen replied sadly, "She didn't say. I came in to see you because I'm about to go off duty and will be on holiday for a week, so I wanted to come in to wish you all the very best and to say that I will see you when I get back."

When I saw Helen a week later she told me that she suspected that I knew exactly what the Consultant was going to say to us. The Consultant came back later in the evening and said, "Shall we go to the relatives' room?" I was in a state of panic; my sixth sense already knew what was going to be said. She told us what we didn't want to hear, "Miracles do occasionally happen but I don't think that in this case one will. There is no way out for Gabrielle other than death, we have done everything humanly possible for her. There are too many things wrong that can't possibly be put right." I didn't want to hear this. I bowed my head and tried to stop uncontrollable sobs and snorts coming from my tortured body.

"Gabrielle needs a hundred percent oxygen to breathe and there is no way of telling what has happened to her brain or why she had the fits." She carried on speaking but her words were fading into the background. The Consultant was really very nice and had great difficulty in telling us all this, she had grown fond of Gabrielle herself, the entire regular nursing staff had, after all we had been there almost six months. She said that even without all these complications there were no guarantees that all would have ended well with Gabrielle's gut, even though it appeared to be going well – it was a serious gut problem.

When my mind was able to focus on her voice again I could hear her as she continued, "You have two options open to you. You can either leave things as they are and eventually Gabrielle's heart will find it too much and it will give up. There is no way of knowing how long it will take; her potassium levels are dangerously high and that will cause her heart to fail. Or, you could have the ventilator switched off which would mean that you would be able to dress Gabrielle and hug her until she dies. There is no rush to make a decision either way, take your time. No matter what, Gabrielle will not suffer because she is sedated and has morphine to stop any pain – which will not be taken away."

We believed that Gabrielle's Consultant and her team had done everything they could and we were faced with the worst decision a parent would ever have to make. Donald and I had already had this theoretical discussion, 'what we would do if.' We had decided that we thought it best in this type of situation that the next of kin should have the ventilator switched off. The theoretical situation for us had now become a reality.

I hadn't been able to speak since we went into that room. The tears were rolling down my face. I felt beaten, let down and I was heaving and really wanted to be sick, not with food though. I wanted to spew out my guts. My heart was shattered into a million pieces. Donald and I were holding on to each other. Donald said, "We'll turn the ventilator off."

"Are you sure it's want you both want?" Gabrielle's Consultant looked at me; she wanted assurance that it was what we both wanted. I had no words, so nodded.

Donald took control for both of us and told her, "There is no point in prolonging it any longer than necessary, so we'll let the family know and do it tonight."

"Take your time, there is no rush. I'm so very sorry the outcome couldn't have been different." She smiled kindly at us and rested her hand on my shoulder once again, before leaving the room.

Donald telephoned the families and told them the situation. Donald's family said that they would like to remember Gabrielle as they last saw her so wouldn't come unless we wanted them to. My Mum said she wanted to come and see her one last time. I didn't really want to be waiting around for another hour for them to arrive, I just wanted to get it over with, but we had given them the option, so had to let them come. Donald also let Faye know.

While we were waiting, Donald and Samantha's Dad took all Gabrielle's belongings and put them in the car then emptied our room; we could have stayed there overnight but didn't want to. We gave Gabrielle's ducks to Samantha because she also liked playing with them. While Donald was loading the car, the telephone rang on the ward. One of the nurses called out to me,

"Jeany, it's for you. It's your friend Jane."

I took the telephone, "Hi, Jeany, I thought I'd give you a ring to see how things are going."

I could hear my friends cheerful voice but couldn't speak the huge lump in my throat was so painful and seemed to block my airway. She had no idea what her telephone call had blundered into. "Jeany, are you ok? What's happening?" Jane's voice was so near and yet so far. Panic and question were now obvious in her tone. Donald walked back on to the ward; I thrust the telephone to him and walked away leaving him to explain the situation.

Sylvia had finished her shift and I knew she would want to know what was happening, so I went to the public telephone in the relatives' room and dialled her number, "Hello, Gabrielle's going to die tonight." I blurted out.

"Jeany, Jeany, what did you say?" Sylvia couldn't believe what she had just heard. Then my words began to sink in, "Can I come in Jeany?" She asked me softly. I couldn't talk and handed the receiver to Samantha's Mum.

Afterwards she sat with me and we waited. I continued to heave uncontrollably and wished that if things couldn't get better it would be over.

At last my Mum arrived with my stepfather and one of my brothers they were all crying. My Mum threw her arms around me, "All week I've wanted to be near you." We stood there hugging before I took them through to see Gabrielle to say their goodbyes.

I had seen Sister Esther on the ward earlier and asked if she was still around. She was and so I asked her to be with us and pray.

We then got Gabrielle ready. Mel (a sister on the ward and Gabrielle's nurse for the night) helped me to give her a wash and put Johnson's baby mousse oil all over her. Donald and I chose a new blue and white sailor dress that one of my sisters had just bought for her. We chose it because she hadn't had the chance to wear it yet together with a white cardigan that I had knitted for her – so that she wouldn't get cold. We completed her outfit with white lacy tights and her pink furry slippers that my Mum had bought.

When we had finished, Gabrielle looked more like herself. All the time I was washing and dressing her I talked to her, told her that I loved her with all my heart and that I didn't want to let her go but I had no other choice. She had obviously had enough, she'd lost the fight and was going to go to heaven and live with God. He had created her and now he was taking her away.

Two records by Gloria Estefan had played on the radio all that week, "Can't stay away from you" and "Anything for you". They were so apt and described so many of my feelings.

They inspired a letter I wrote to Gabrielle which I have included later in the book.

Mel took away everything except the morphine and ventilator, there was somewhere around twenty sockets in the wall – everyone being used with either a monitor or a machine for putting drugs into our little girl.

Gabrielle's Consultant came round again and spoke to the nursing staff and us. She was so very sorry. She once again placed her hand reassuringly on my shoulder before she left.

The nurses always find death difficult, but usually they can be detached because they don't have the babies in for very long so don't get to know them or the parents. Our situation was different; most of them had known us for six months and had obviously grown attached to us all. Mel cut a few strands of Gabrielle's hair off for me and put them in a little pot. She couldn't get much because it had been shaved so often. I put her blood-stained mittens and bootees in a little plastic bag and kept them separate from everything else.

"Jeany...." Donald's voice was a distant sound in my mind, "Jeany...." When Gabrielle was dressed, Donald took her in his arms and cuddled her then handed her to me. We were crying, the nurses were crying. It was so awful. I still kept heaving, I felt as though I was going to turn inside out. Sister Esther came and laid her hand on Gabrielle's head and prayed. I don't know what she said; I don't know what was going on around me apart from all the hurt. It was such a horrible feeling, there, in my arms, was a part of me and before long she would be gone forever and I would never be able to hold her, touch her, kiss her, play with her, look at her, talk to her, soothe her or anything else – ever again.

An icy silence hung in the air.

"Jeany....." Donald was persistent in trying to get my attention, "JEANY...." his voice faded into my conscious. Donald was talking to me but I didn't hear what he said at first, I was too wrapped up in my own thoughts. Then I realised. "Are you ready, Jeany?"

"SHUT UP!" I yelled. I didn't want to hear what he was saying.

"Come on Jeany. We've got to do this. Are you ready?"

"I've told you to shut up!"

Donald was holding me and stroking Gabrielle. I knew what he was asking me. I wasn't ready. I would never be ready. How can a mother ever be ready to take the breath away from her child? I knew it had to be done eventually, but I just DIDN'T WANT to do it. I just couldn't agree with him. This day had always been there, tucked away in the archives of my mind from the very beginning, but I had hoped and prayed that we would never have to face it and here we were.

It was worse than I had ever imagined it could be.

Donald kept repeating my name, to try to get me back to reality. I tensed, and clenched my whole body. I would <u>never</u> be ready to allow my baby to die. NEVER! I wanted to hold Gabrielle forever. All the time that ventilator was in place she had breath and so was alive. She didn't have a life, but she was alive. I don't know how long we cuddled Gabrielle but it wasn't long enough and never would be.

Eventually Donald turned to Mel, "It's time. Do it." He choked. He knew that I wouldn't say it; Mel knew it was what we had both agreed, but still needed me to say that I was ready.

"Jeany?" she enquired. I barely nodded.

Mel removed the ventilator from Gabrielle's throat, leaving only the morphine drip to ensure that Gabrielle suffered no pain.

"Will it take long?" I whispered.

"No." Mel replied gently. "Gabrielle has so much pressure on her lungs with all the fluid that she won't be able to breathe." I cradled Gabrielle in my arms and Donald had one of his arms around me and the other around her. I watched helplessly as Gabrielle breathed her last breaths.

We told her that we loved her over and over and said goodbye to her too as she slipped quietly away in my arms.

I just didn't know what to do with myself. What do you do when you have created a part of yourself, had her inside your womb all those months, gone through absolute agony to give birth to her, then had all the joy that new life brings for six months only to have it end so tragically, watching her die in your arms? I had wanted children for as long as I could remember and as soon as I found out that I was pregnant, I loved this child that had been created with love. When we found out that she had a problem during the pregnancy I loved her more and as time went on – my love increased. I never thought it possible that I could love someone so much or that I could hurt so much.

During this last week as Gabrielle lay there dying, so too did a part of me. My heart was broken; part of it died and Gabrielle took it with her. I don't want it back as it belongs with her. I laid Gabrielle on the bed and stormed off to the toilet. "There are so many wicked bastards in the world so why did God have to take my beautiful, innocent Gabrielle? It's just not fair!" I slammed the door, leaned against the wall, thrust my head backwards into the wall, and closed my eyes. My shattered heart felt as though it was going to burst up through my throat – if it had I would have walked away and left it to rot on the floor – I had no need of it now.

Why should it be this way? Our faith had really taken a battering over these last six months. Our whole lives had changed and we'd had hardly any time for each other because we were either at the hospital, travelling or too tired for anything other than getting as much sleep as we could. I know that God is not to blame for this. We live on earth where things aren't fair; if everything was great here then we'd have nothing to look forward to. But I wanted to know why I had such a raw deal out of life. This was the icing on the cake for me. I know that her condition was one in ninety thousand, but to me she was one in more than a hundred million – more than I knew how to count and neither Donald nor I would ever have changed her. Why did she have to have this rare condition? I thought that it was maybe to give Donald the daughter he wanted and then by her death God was protecting her because I wouldn't have been able to save her from the hands of my stepfather, just as my Mum had not protected me. Donald had absolutely no idea what had happened with my stepfather so he had no such concerns. It didn't make any more sense than the rest of it.

I went back on to the ward to see my baby again. Everyone was upset and kind to me. My body was ripped to shreds and if it wasn't for having Donald, I would have made sure that I had died too.

It was so hard to leave Gabrielle there and go home, knowing that I would never see her again. I couldn't comprehend that she wouldn't be there when we returned in the morning. I don't know what time we left or how long it took us to get home – even how we managed to get home. I do know that neither of us slept that night, our world had been shattered and had come crashing down around us.

The next morning we decided to go to the doctors and get some sleeping tablets. Unfortunately our own doctor was on holiday so we saw her partner. The hospital had already telephoned the surgery to let them know what had happened so when we asked for sleeping tablets, that's what we expected to get; but this woman decided to give us a chat. "You should go away for a holiday, and while you are away, ask someone to go into your house and rearrange the furniture." the voice came from the other side of the desk. "Forget about what has happened, put it all behind you, throw away the pictures and start again. I know someone who's ten year old has just been run over and killed which is worse than what has happened to you."

Donald spoke a little to her but she turned to me and said, "You aren't saying anything."

"I have nothing to say to you!" I spat at her. I couldn't wait to leave – in fact, I really wanted to slap her! We took the prescription and left.

We then drove back to London to pick up the death certificate so that we could register Gabrielle's death. Alison hadn't been there the night before. When she came on duty with the other nurses, the news was broken to them. They were all so kind and were horrified when we told them about our experience with the G.P. and they wanted to complain on our behalf. They said that they could have given us some sleeping tablets from one of their doctors had we asked. Alison told us that we had to register the death in Bow Register Office, it's a good job she did because otherwise we'd have gone back to our home town to do it.

I kept looking at the space where only hours before we had been and our little girl had died. We had a chat with the nurses and promised to keep in touch, then left for the Register Office.

On the death certificate it said that Gabrielle had died of: -

1. Respiratory Arrest

   a. Pulmonary Oedema

2. Renal Failure

3. Short Bowel Syndrome, Hepatic Failure

Chapter 16

The Worst Days of My Life

Donald dropped me off and went to park the car. I was shown into a room and a man began to ask me questions, but as soon as Donald arrived I left him to answer the rest of them.

The man behind the desk handed me a pen, "Can you please sign there?"

"What is it?" I questioned.

"The Death Certificate."

I screamed at him, "No! He can sign it".

"I'm sorry, but I have put you down as the informant now," the Registrar kindly explained, "so I do need you to sign it."

I picked up the pen with a trembling hand, hovered over the Certificate, then threw it across the table, and screamed out, "I signed the consent form for the operation that killed her, and I don't want to sign the death certificate, too! He signed all the successful operation forms and the Birth Certificate. I don't want to be the one to sign the operation causing her death AND the Death Certificate."

Donald held on to me, "Please, Jeany. You have to sign it. It's not your fault, but you do have to sign it." Shaking, I picked up the pen, threw it back again before eventually being able to bring myself to put my signature to the Death Certificate. I realised that I had no choice, but really didn't want to do it. Had I thought for one moment that this would happen I would have waited outside for Donald to come back from parking the car. Donald was so lovely to me and held on to me as I signed the form.

We headed home armed with the information to give to the funeral director. Back to the cold, empty house where we just existed. We had a big decision to make next. Do we bury Gabrielle or have her cremated? We went to the crematorium to enquire about both. It didn't seem possible that on this day four years before we went out for a meal together to celebrate our engagement when Donald had placed a shining solitaire diamond ring on my finger. How our emotions were so different.

It seemed that if we chose burial, we would have to decide if we wanted a family plot or a plot just for Gabrielle, if we had a cremation there was a special flower bed just for children. We sat on a bench in the grounds talking about what we thought would be best. Donald had always favoured cremations, but my grandparents had been buried, so even though he would prefer a cremation he would go along with whatever I wanted. Eventually we decided that a cremation would be the best option, we may not always be around to ensure that a grave would be well kept, whereas the crematorium staff keep the gardens tidy and weeded. We didn't like the idea of booking a family plot or having Gabrielle buried on her own.

We went to make the arrangements. The lady at the Funeral Directors was really nice and very helpful. We gave her the paperwork, which included the authority to bring Gabrielle back home, and she asked us if we would want to see Gabrielle before the funeral. We weren't sure so she left it open for us. What I did know was that I didn't want anybody else to see her.

Donald didn't really feel the need to go to see Gabrielle but I did. I wanted to make sure that they had brought the right person back from London, so Donald said that he'd come with me.

We had to choose a posy; the florist had a colour brochure of all the different designs. Donald chose the one he liked. "Why did you choose that one?" I asked.

"The ribbons circling the outside of the posy remind me one of Gabrielle's dresses that I liked her wearing." I could barely keep control of myself. Donald didn't often express opinions like that so as far as I was concerned – we had to have that one.

I don't remember much else about what we did apart from Donald driving through a red light and not even realising that he had done it. We could have been killed if something had been coming the other way but we wouldn't have really cared at that point.

The day before the funeral we went to see Gabrielle in the chapel of rest. I took a teddy to put in the coffin, not her favourite one because it had a bell in it and I wasn't sure if it was allowed, but as she always loved to cuddle a teddy I wanted her to have one with her. She looked better than she had when she had died, because the swelling had gone down.

There was a chair to the side so Donald went and sat on it while I looked under the pretty cover to make sure Gabrielle still had her slippers on. "They are there Donald, but I wish...I...hadn't..." I sensed that Donald wasn't listening so looked across at him. He had his head in his hands and was crying. I walked over and stood in front of him, he put his arms around my middle, and we cried together as I stroked his hair.

This would definitely be the last time we would ever see Gabrielle so I didn't want to leave, the last time we would see her flesh, be able to touch her skin and kiss her – we had seemed to cry so much – it was never ending. Eventually we kissed her goodbye and went back home to wait for the funeral.

The morning of the funeral dawned. Faye sent Amy to Owens' Mum so that they could prepare the food for the funeral for us. Donald and I were just 'dangling' not knowing what to do, dreading every second of the day. We had asked that people donate money for a machine we wanted to buy in memory of Gabrielle, which would help others, instead of buying flowers; but flowers <u>and</u> money poured in. Then people began to arrive and as the time drew nearer I began to get more and more uptight thinking that the funeral directors would be late. We had been given the option of meeting them at the crematorium but we wanted Gabrielle to go from home. A home that she had never known, nevertheless it was still her home and she had lived there, inside me, for seven and a half months. Her bedroom was here, all her belongings were here, and so were all her family. Today her house was also filled with her friends and most of the nurses that had cared for her in the hospital.

The cars came round, and the funeral director collected up all the flowers. Ours went on top of her coffin. We got into the car. I made sure that I got in first and Donald followed me so that I didn't have to sit next to anyone but him. I only wanted Donald, my husband and the father of my child.

I knew that Donald's shift was going to the funeral but I wasn't prepared for what I saw. At the end of our road was one of his colleagues, who stopped all the traffic and saluted Gabrielle and the funeral procession before allowing the traffic to flow again. There were others along the route including at the crematorium entrance saluting us – I almost choked trying to remain in control at each one. I was told, but didn't see it for myself; the rest of the shift got out of the minibus and marched in formation across to the chapel.

Even now, many years down the line; every time I think about those loyal and supportive colleagues saluting our daughter, it fills me with tears and I fight to remain in control.

A very young funeral director carried Gabrielle's coffin in his arms, close to his chest into the chapel and we followed. James did a lovely service although I cannot remember that much about it. We sang "The Day Thou Gavest" and "Bind us Together". We had "Bind us Together" at our Wedding and I was always singing it to Gabrielle, adding in an extra verse about binding the two of us together.

How I managed to get through the service I will never know. I didn't cry, but I shook from head to toe uncontrollably. I thought that I was going to collapse when it came to the coffin being taken away. I wanted to rush up to Gabrielle, throw myself onto her and not let her go. I wanted to scream out, tell them to give me my baby back, I wanted her home and I knew that this was the last ever physical thing left of her and that was about to be taken way. I would have gladly gone into the furnace with her. I didn't want them to take her away. I began heaving all over again and just could not stop shaking. What was I going to do? How could I live on? I wanted my baby so desperately and knew that I would never have her again. I had to hang on to Donald for support so that I didn't end up in a heap on the floor.

Everyone commented on how strong Donald and I had been that day, but we certainly didn't feel it. We went round to look at the flowers; there were loads and I was amazed to see so many people there also. People I used to work with before I had Gabrielle, and so many of our friends and family that hadn't come to the house first, as well as the nurses, Samantha's parents and many other people. Gabrielle's Consultant had sent us a lovely letter and the nurses told us that she had not done that before to any other parents.

When it was all over and everyone had gone home, Faye and Owen insisted we go in to their house for dinner. I didn't want to eat and just wanted to shut myself away from the world, but they wouldn't let me.

We were told by a lot of people that they would leave us to grieve in peace and that we should contact them when we were ready. That's not really a good thing to say, I now understand that they didn't know what to say as almost every topic of conversation could inadvertently have hurt us. I have since learnt that what grieving people need are not words but friends who will listen, hold their hands and not necessarily say a word.

With all the flowers we received, I didn't think that we would have raised much money for the hospital but we did. The donations bought a new computerised drip machine with money to spare, and the hospital had a plaque put on it in Gabrielle's memory. She had been using the only two on the ward, and they wanted to replace all their old ones with the new computerized machines. The total amount raised in gifts and donations was £1,567.73 which at the time was about two months average earnings.

Our parents encouraged us to spend some time away and they helped towards the cost of it, too. So a few days after the funeral we went for a midweek break to try to pick up the threads of our lives. We hadn't realised how much stress we had been under for so long until we were away from it all. We spent some time in tears and it dawned on us how little time we'd had for each other during the last six months. Now it was just Jeany and Donald together twenty-four hours a day.

One night we made love – something we hadn't done for so long as it either hadn't seemed right, or we just didn't have the time or the energy – but that night, it was something magical and really special and it released so much tension from both of us.

When we got back we had Gabrielle's ashes interred alongside the rose bush we had chosen for her in the children's flower bed. It was a cold blustery day and we decided that there would only be James and the two of us there. We also had to decide what we wanted written on the plaque for the rose and a verse to go in the book in the Memorial Chapel. Donald couldn't do it, so I spent hours trying to find the right words before I was satisfied and Donald agreed with what I had written.

How could I carry on now? How could I live again? I thought that I'd found happiness when I married Donald and very quickly became pregnant, even considering the shock of knowing that something was wrong with our baby – I never thought in my wildest imagination, that Gabrielle would die. Why was life so cruel? Hadn't I suffered enough before I married Donald? The world seemed to stop.

Chapter 17

Learning to Live Again

We had to learn to live again – life had to go on. Many well meaning people gave us advice on what to do next, how long we should wait before having another baby. We made the decision to have another baby as soon as possible and it just so happened that my packet of contraceptive pills finished the same day as Gabrielle's funeral, so we didn't take any further precautions.

We could never replace our darling daughter and we didn't want to, but were sure that she would like brothers or sisters to add to our family.

I had my monthly period after stopping the pills, and I thought that I would have become pregnant – after all I'd fallen the first time with Gabrielle. When my next period arrived I was devastated, "That's it! I'll never become pregnant again!" I sat there, my head in my hands, "I've had my chance and now it's gone. I'll never be a pregnant again." Donald took my hands in his, drew me up to him and held me tightly in his arms.

"It's only been one month, Jeany. We can't expect it to happen straight away." His voice was gentle and reassuring.

"But it did last time!" I protested. Donald sighed, not really knowing what to do or say next.

The following month my heart leapt when I didn't get my period. I bought a test to do so that I could surprise Donald with the result – it was negative. A couple of weeks later there was still no sign of my period, so I did the second test – again it was negative so I was convinced I'd remain childless and became quite depressed.

We went north to stay with Donald's God-parents for a week in June. We had wine every night with dinner – I had nothing to lose, but half way through the week I still had no period and got really upset. "I haven't had a period, I know not pregnant, yet I feel that I am and I don't know what to do Donald!" I gabbled.

He comforted me, "We can buy a test and do it as soon as we get home."

"There's no point I've already done two and they both came up negative!"I despaired

"So we'll do a third." I stopped drinking the wine.

As soon as we got home, we did the test. It was POSITIVE – I was having another baby! Panic arose within me out of nowhere. What would happen next? How would I cope?

Donald and I talked about the "what if's". Could we go through it all again? I didn't know that I could go through with an abortion either, I was petrified. I was desperate for another child, but I wanted it to be a healthy child. My emotions were all over the place and I wasn't really sure about anything.

I went to my GP who referred me to the hospital immediately. The first time we saw our baby I was about eight weeks pregnant and all we could see was a tiny muscle moving – it was the baby's heart beating. We had so many scans that I lost count. My consultant wanted to do his best to reassure me that all was well "as far as they could see" but I would not be convinced.

We followed all the stages of the pregnancy in the book, just as we had with Gabrielle, and began to get to know our new baby. I had lots of extra check-ups with the GP, Midwife and at the hospital – everyone was so very understanding and caring.

According to my dates, GP and Midwife, our baby was due in March. It meant a Christmas with no children – a thought which filled me with dread, as did the thought that the baby would be late and arrive on the date of Gabrielle's death. My consultant assured me he would do all he could for that not to happen, BUT, the scans gave a due date within three days of this event. I totally disagreed with that date; however, the scan date was the date everything went by.

The due date came and went, as did every day for the following week. I was really beginning to panic, my consultant told me that if the baby hadn't arrived by ten days after the scan date I would go in to be induced, but he'd rather not take that course due to the fact that I'd had a caesarean with Gabrielle.

To my horror another week came and went which contained the anniversary of Gabrielle's death. Gabrielle had been dead one year. How it hurt, how very much it hurt. It had hurt me throughout the year and I'd spent many hours sitting up at the crematorium talking to Gabrielle – the pleasure and joy of being pregnant and looking forward to the birth of our second child was marred with the raw pain I still felt. I prayed like mad, that it would not arrive on this day.

Three days later, just as Donald was dishing up the tea, my waters broke and we were off to the hospital for our baby to be born. After only four hours and five minutes of labour, Megan Louise entered the world weighing eight pounds, five ounces. I looked at the shape of her head and whispered to Donald, "Do you think she's mentally handicapped?" Unbeknown to me the midwife had heard my words to Donald.

Turning to me she said, "My dear, Gabrielle was born by caesarean and Megan has just squashed through a birth canal so her head is bound to be misshapen, it will soon settle down."

Megan's hands and feet were dried, cracked and bleeding a sure sign of an over cooked baby!

Terror struck me once again when Megan constantly vomited while still attached to my breast and feeding, I thought that she must have a problem with her guts, but the midwives assured me that she was just being greedy. To try to reassure me they called the doctors to examine her who confirmed it.

Five days later she had settled down and we were allowed to go home.

Chapter 18

Our Completed Family

Donald became desperate for another baby when Megan was about six months old but I wasn't keen. "It seems that I've been either pregnant or breast feeding every Christmas since we've married, so can't we wait until after Christmas?" I pleaded.

After Christmas I was still worried. I wanted to wait a bit longer, because I couldn't face having another pregnancy during the same months I had carried Gabrielle. Donald reluctantly agreed, but then the first time we "tried" after that, I found myself pregnant. Panic filled me once again I already had a baby; Megan wasn't a year old – how would I cope? I'd had one baby die, the other was alive; which would this next baby be, dead or alive?

I coped with the pregnancy better than I thought once again having more scans than usual. One day in December I woke in the early hours of the morning with pains similar to that of period pains. I did my best to push them to the back of my mind and later that day we took Megan to her Pre-school Bazaar, all the while my back was really aching. "I wouldn't be surprised if this baby comes today, Donald." I remarked rubbing my back as Megan excitedly headed for Santa.

"Uhuh!" Donald pondered, not really paying much attention.

Donald went to work at four o'clock in the afternoon and I told him to be ready to come home at a moments' notice. His parents came to see me and Donald's Mum, Ginny, did my ironing and helped me with the housework. "Have you got any twinges yet?" Ginny enquired.

"Do you think I would say if I had?" I was having irregular contractions, but covered them up. I didn't want anyone to know I was in pain.

"Knowing you? No, I don't suppose you would." Ginny smiled.

Time moved on and Donald's Dad, Henry read Megan a bedtime story and we settled her down to sleep. "What time is Donald due home?" Ginny asked.

"Not until midnight." I answered.

"You look tired, Jeany. Do you want to go up to bed and we'll wait here until Donald gets home?"

"No, it's okay thanks. I'll be alright."

"We'll go then – if you're sure you don't need us – but on one condition," Ginny said kindly, "that you go up to bed because you look extremely tired."

Not long after they had gone the contractions very quickly became more intense and frequent.

At about half past nine I called Donald. I tried to keep my voice as calm as possible,

"You'd better come home as I'm having lots of contractions and they're coming quite frequently." I went upstairs and sat on Megan's bed, it was only a single bed, but she looked lost in it. At only twenty months old, I didn't want to leave her behind, nor wake her now but I also didn't want her to wake up in the morning and find that I was gone.

As she lay sleeping I kissed her and as I stroked her hair I whispered in her ear, "Mummy loves you babe. I'm off to the hospital now to have the baby. I love you!"

Faye came in to look after Megan and Donald drove me through the fog to the hospital where at eleven twenty-five, Elizabeth Victoria shot into the world weighing eight pounds, three ounces!

Panic and fear struck once again when Elizabeth was jaundice and had to go under the ultra-violet lamp, laying there with a bandage blindfolding her – she looked just like Gabrielle. Was life ever going to get any easier for me?

Donald came in the next day with Megan. She sat on my bed and tapped her lap to cuddle the baby. She had always said she wanted a baby sister and so had her wish. As Megan cradled Elizabeth she said, "Mummy, baby, come home now!" This was a huge sentence for a twenty month old.

I was filled with love and tears. Throughout my pregnancy I had explained to Megan that one day Mummy would go to the hospital, the nurse would get the baby out and then she would come to the hospital with Daddy and take me home. I had no idea she had actually really understood what I'd been saying to her.

"The baby's poorly at the moment, darling, so we can't come home just yet." I told her. My Mum came to stay to look after Megan and Donald while I was in hospital. Megan loved it and refused to have anything to do with me when they came into the hospital; she cuddled Elizabeth and my Mum. This was alien to me. Megan usually couldn't get enough cuddles from me. She didn't like other people hugging her and yet here she was completely ignoring me. Didn't she love me anymore? Concern must have shown on my face. "Don't worry love," said my Mum, "she confused and she will come round."

I think that Megan wasn't happy that I had broken my word but five days later – the day she and Donald came to pick me up from the hospital, she would not leave me alone. She sat cuddling me at every opportunity.

We were under constant threat of going back into hospital because the jaundice hadn't cleared. To our great relief and happiness a few days later it did and we were reprieved. We had two beautiful daughters who gave us joy, pleasure, fun, laughter, tears and pain, but it was all normal, at last we could live. They helped us with the pain and searing loss we had felt with losing Gabrielle, BUT my life was far from settled. I became very depressed.

Chapter 19

Talking at Last!

When Elizabeth reached the time of her nine month hearing check, I couldn't hold it inside any longer I had to tell someone before I burst. My health visitor had changed and the new one offered to come round and chat with me but she didn't come quickly enough – I really needed to talk. I was at the end of my tether and didn't know which way to turn so rather than go to my local clinic, I took Elizabeth to be weighed at a clinic where my Health Visitor, Annette, was more likely to be.

My emotions were mixed, I was elated that she was there, and yet absolutely petrified. In my head I was constantly praying that I would get to speak to her and that I would have the courage to ask her to come round. I did. She visited me one afternoon and miraculously both girls fell asleep. I was terrified that I would lose my girls and my husband because of what I had done many years ago. I didn't deserve to be happy. I began by asking her, "If I told you something, who would you tell?" Annette paused before replying.

"If you tell me something which meant that a child was in danger, I would have to tell my supervisor and decide on a course of action to take, but I can't think of anything else off the top of my head that would mean I would have to take it any further – it could remain confidential between the two of us." I began to talk about my childhood, it was the first time I had been able to talk to anyone but it began many years of more trauma and heartache.

I felt that I wanted to smash my head against the brick wall. I'd had enough of listening to my Mum talking to the girls and saying that they could go to stay with her. As I write this decades on, I am moved to tears because I feel so upset at the fact that I denied my Mum this pleasure, and the pleasure of even looking after them without me for a short period of time, but I just couldn't take the chance that our girls would suffer at the hands of her husband as I had. I had to protect them at all costs after all, only I could do it.

My depression took an even crueller twist. I constantly accused Donald of not caring about Gabrielle, saying that because he never brought her name up it must mean that he didn't care anymore and didn't love her. I plunged deeper and deeper into depression. I felt that I couldn't cope with looking after myself, let alone our two girls and Donald. I was most definitely at the bottom of a downward spiral staircase and dare not even look up let alone know how to get back up again.

I had recurring nightmares, just as when I was a child. I dreamt that I went to the hospital to see Gabrielle, she had been there all these years, but I just hadn't gone to visit her. She was grown up yet still a baby and I felt gutted that I hadn't visited her all through the years and yet relief washed over me because it meant Gabrielle was alive! Suddenly, I'd wake up with two very painful thoughts and feelings tearing through my body, mind and soul. Physical pain and emotional despair that I had not visited our darling daughter for so many years and had left her alone in hospital, mixed with relief that she was still alive. Then the ten ton truck hit me and I was trapped underneath it, the weight and the pain was too much to bear.

It had been a dream, the glimmer of hope that I'd not lost my baby after all was shattered, Gabrielle really was dead and there was no going back to the hospital to visit her – she was gone forever.

Another recurring nightmare was that Donald and I were married but he had not found us a home to live in so we were living in my parents' house with the girls. We had no privacy and I felt as though I would suffocate with the pressure. Sometimes the venue changed and we were all living in our house, but it still wasn't ours, it still belonged to my parents. The nightmare seemed to last forever and when I woke up I was so relieved to find that I was in our home, and it was our home.

My depression continued and one day Donald lost his temper with me for the way I was behaving, "I lost Gabrielle too!" he despaired at me. He didn't know that it was far more than that. How could I tell him? He had such a good relationship with my family, I couldn't destroy that. But how else could I protect our girls?

Chapter 20

Donald & I

Donald I started going out together when we were in our late teens. We'd lived in the neighbourhood for about eight years and went to the same school. Donald used to go to church twice a month to qualify to go to the weekly youth club. He and his mates wanted to go to the youth club because that's where the girls were! Suddenly I began to notice this young man passing my house every Monday and I wanted to get to know him better.

Every Monday I would strain to look out of my bedroom window to see when Donald was approaching, and then I would rush down the stairs and "accidently bump into him" at the end of my driveway. We would walk the ten or fifteen minute journey to the local shopping parade where he would turn left to take his bus to his day release college course and I would turn right for my bus to the college where I was studying a bi-lingual secretary course.

Some weeks later my stepfather, who knew that Donald loved to tinker with cars, asked him if he would like to help get my 'old banger' on the road and Donald jumped at the chance. I became surprisingly interested in car mechanics and 'helped' as much as I could. I actually learned a lot.

Now and again, Donald would 'accidently' make physical contact with me, his hand would rest on mine or he'd lean across me, and once he even stole a peck on the cheek. I found myself wanting more of it and would put myself in positions where he could 'accidently' make some sort of physical contact. These feelings were new to me as I'd only known abuse. I'd never wanted any sort of physical contact with a member of the opposite sex before, and yet here I was engineering it!

Donald asked my stepfather's permission to take my sister and me out to the fair ground and such like. I began to get a bit confused because I thought he liked me and felt sure we would become 'an item'. Donald managed an increasing number of pecks on my cheek, and yet he didn't seem to take it any further. I made up my mind that I wasn't going to let him do it again and yet I wanted him to because it felt so comfortable.

One evening, my sister, a friend, Donald and I went to a disco. Donald and I spent the evening drinking and talking then at the end of the evening they played "The Last Waltz". Donald asked me if I wanted to dance. It wasn't a waltz, it was merely the two of us hanging on to each other and barely moving on the dance floor. I remember saying to Donald, "Are we two lonely people together?" but don't remember what he replied. We got back to my house and leant on the bonnet of my car where we had the most incredible kiss. It was just like it was in all those old fashioned romantic movies and I never wanted it to end. We came up for air, "Will you go out with me, Jeany and be mine?"

"Of course I will." My heart was bursting with joy.

Our lips locked together. It was about an hour later I went indoors and Donald went home.

A short while after that I announced to Donald that I didn't believe in sex before marriage. Four factors influenced my stating this to him. First of all I believed that as a Christian sex outside of marriage was wrong. Secondly, my Mum made no secret of the fact that she believed that marriage was the place for sex and I didn't want to let her down. Thirdly I wanted to be in control of sex and finally I wanted to see how far I could push Donald before he either tried to force me into sex or dumped me because I wouldn't give it to him. To my amazement, he accepted it and still wanted to be with me! I couldn't believe it, this was so alien. How could anyone like him want me anyway? He always had girls flocking around him and everyone wanted to be 'Donald's Girl'! Apart from anything else, in my bid to protect myself, and in particular to be unattractive to my stepfather, I was quite the tomboy and I thought ugly.

I wanted to be with Donald all the time and yet I constantly tested him to see how far I could push him before he left me or tried to force me into anything I didn't want to do. He never did. He was so kind, caring and considerate, kept his hands to himself and even didn't try to make me do anything to him. He was happy to do whatever I wanted to do or go wherever I wanted to go. Our relationship was built on conversation and laughter – I was never happier.

Things changed for me at home with my stepfather, he and Donald became good friends and Donald often worked with him.

Over the years I tried to put Donald off and felt like ending the relationship many times. I felt insecure and wanted to hurt him before he could hurt me, but all that happened was that we grew stronger. When Donald told me he loved me, surprisingly I snapped at him, "Don't say that, you don't know what you are talking about!"

"Okay," replied Donald calmly. He did as I asked and stopped telling me, but then I missed it. More importantly he showed me that he loved me by his actions.

A year or two went by and one night with the 'security blanket' of darkness, I asked Donald if he had ever wondered why I made no effort to touch him intimately. He replied that he did wonder but that he didn't want to force me into anything I didn't want to do. I didn't feel confident enough, given Donald's friendship with my stepfather, to tell Donald about the abuse my stepfather had subject me to. So I told him about my experience with my Grandad and I gave him the chance to finish with me. He didn't want to, so I asked him to help me to overcome my fears as long as he was prepared to be patient and take things completely at my pace.

The years passed, and in December we decided to get engaged with the view to being married a couple of years' later. Donald spoke to my stepfather about it and then, on 31ˢᵗ December, as we welcomed in the New Year, Donald announced to my family our intention to marry. My Mum burst into tears, "I thought you were just friends. He's younger than you. Your father was younger than me and look what happened to me. Donald hasn't had his flings yet, so he'll do it after you are married like your father did!" Mum cried.

Yes, we had known each other as friends since we were children but we had been going out together for over three years by this time. Mum was going by her own experience with my Dad, or at least how she perceived it. This is totally understandable as we only have our experiences to learn by, but how could I explain the comments I'd made to Donald and his reactions to them? If Donald had wanted a sex filled relationship he'd have left me a long time ago. At the beginning of our relationship there was absolutely no intimate contact, I had told him about my Grandad, which hadn't put him off. He had spent the following years helping me through it with no pressure and despite everything; we still had not had full sexual relations over three years into our relationship. Everything we did in our lives together felt so right, so much so that I had stopped thinking about all the things that had happened to me before. All that mattered now was Donald and I being together, and marriage couldn't come around quickly enough for me. I knew that 'having flings' would not be on Donald's agenda or mine.

Mum quickly came around to the idea of our marriage. I would come home from work to find little bits and bobs on my bed towards my "bottom drawer". I believe that my Mum's initial reaction was one borne out of fear from her own experiences.

Our wedding date was set. We had planned a seated buffet followed by a disco, with a seven day honeymoon in Gran Canarias. There were the usual 'wedding differences of opinion' between our families, but eventually everything was set and booked.

During the week before our wedding day we went to the caterers, who were friends of my late Grandparents. We paid them the balance and told them that my stepfather said that if they needed a hand to transport the food on Saturday to give him a ring.

Just before our special day our vicar became so ill that his doctor wanted him to go to hospital and get a locum to perform our ceremony, but he refused. He'd been looking forward to our wedding day. The reason was most of the young people we had grown up with had partners from outside the church, but we were the only "home grown" couple.

Our wedding day dawned. My stepfather, sisters and I went to decorate the church hall for the reception, when all of a sudden my Mum appeared, flustered and in a blind panic. She went up to my stepfather and whispered something to him. I heard him say in a loud voice, "Well you'd better tell her, you can't keep it a secret!" Turning to me with a look of panic on her face my Mum exclaimed,

"The caterers thought you were getting married on Nana's wedding anniversary in two weeks' time, not on her birthday. There's no food!"

"Oh!" was all I could manage. I didn't know what else to say.

By the time Mum arrived to tell us about the mix up she had already made some frantic phone calls. "Various friends around the town are preparing some food this morning in the hope that we get enough by this afternoon." Mum rushed away again to co-ordinate more food supplies. Stunned I left the hall and went into the church.

Standing there alone I held out my hands. I said to God, "Why now? What is going on? I thought everything would be so special and I was going to marry the man I loved, the only man who truly loved me. I can't believe what is happening. Is it a sign not to do it or do I press on regardless?" Peace surrounded me and hung in the air, so I left it in God's hands and went back to the hall.

Fortunately the cake had been made by a neighbour and not by the caterers. After decorating the hall I went back home to get my hair done. Donald had to help to transport the cake to the reception. He sat in the back of my stepfather's car carefully balancing a tier on his lap as my stepfather drove to the reception hall. Each layer was taken one by one.

It appeared that God was on my case because fifteen minutes before my wedding food was set out in the hall.

At last we were married, I was so happy; we were very much in love, everything was perfect. Our relationship couldn't have been better and so we intended to start a family as soon as possible.

Chapter 21

The Truth Revealed

A few days after I had spoken to my Health Visitor I was ironing when my friend Sandra telephoned me. I had the telephone tucked under my chin while I was ironing. I confided her and she agreed with my Health Visitor that I had to tell Donald about the abuse I had suffered at the hands of my stepfather.

"But I can't ruin their relationship, they get on so well. How can I shatter Donald's life?" I pleaded.

"Look at it this way then, Jeany. What if Donald was out with the girls, popped in to see your Mum and left the girls there? He'd come back home, you'd go mad and he would feel worse when he realised that he'd put them at risk. You owe it to him." Sandra reasoned. I knew she was right, so I chose my evening.

I was lying on the sofa snuggled in a blanket, but I also needed the security blanket of darkness.

"Donald, I need you to turn the lights out – I have something to tell you. Remember when I told you about my grandad?"

"Yes." Donald said hesitantly.

"Well I…" I stopped talking; I didn't really know what to say. I buried my head into the blanket and remained silent.

"What do you want to tell me, Jeany?" he coaxed.

I lifted my head from the blanket. "I didn't tell you all of it before – there's more."

"Tell me." Donald encouraged,

"I…I…I…please hold me." Donald knelt on the floor by my head; he put one arm under me and the other on top and held me tightly.

"Come on, what do you want to say?"

"No, sorry I can't say it." I buried my head back into the blanket and refused to speak.

"Jeany, you have to tell me. You can't start something like this and not finish it." He pleaded. "Come, on. I've got you. PLEASE tell me."

"What I said happened with my Grandad, also happened with my stepfather only worse, but I don't want to talk about it." I blurted from the depths of the blanket.

Donald released his grip, stood up and backed away from me. I knew it – he didn't want me anymore. The silence froze the air. A few seconds later, after what seemed like an eternity, Donald came back to me and held me again. "I thought you didn't want me anymore," I cried.

"Of course I still want you."

"But you let go and stood up"

"I just wanted to commit murder, HIS murder." I could hear the emotion heavy in his voice.

My sisters had planned to marry so we waited until after their weddings and then went to my parents' house one evening. Mum made a drink and Donald said we needed to talk to them. "We've come to explain why the girls can't come and stay here." I began. My stepfather held my gaze, his eyes daring me not to say anything, so I didn't. I was struck dumb, I doubted myself, gripped with familiar terror.

Donald got angry and shouted, "The girls can't stay with you because things that are unnatural between a father and daughter happened between Jeany and him!" he pointed at my stepfather.

My Mum was livid! My stepfather, still held my gaze before shaking his head and saying,

"Nothing you have suggested has ever happened. You must have misconstrued things."

I looked down to the floor, humiliated, ashamed and filled with fear. My Mum's anger was directed at me. "I'd never have hurt my Mum by telling her something like this. YOU! Should have kept your mouth shut!"

"You should 'effing well listen to your daughter for a change and not HIM!" Donald retorted angrily.

"Oh! Oh! Donald, I never expected you to use the "F" word to me!" exclaimed my Mum, horrified, upset and with fear. Donald took my hand, led me out of the house and took me home.

I was desperate to find something I could give to my Mum to prove that my stepfather was a liar, in the hope that she would begin to believe and support me, so I began to investigate him.

He'd told Mum that he had been married before and that he'd never had children. He also told her of the town that he had lived in during his marriage, and that his parents and his only brother were all dead.

I found his eldest son, his daughter, his Mum and his brother! His daughter had the same name as my half-sister. Through them, I learned many things about my stepfather that confirmed the kind of man I knew he was.

Next I got in touch with the council. When I began working, I had been "asked" to use my wages to enable my stepfather to buy their council house. There were various other documents over the years I was given to sign, without being allowed to read them. I found out that their house was on the verge of being repossessed and that they had further loans against the house. My stepfather also had several dates of birth, none of which were correct. The council sent me copies of some paperwork, but there was too much to send it all!

I took the documentation to show my Mum, but my stepfather talked his way out of it all. "I've never received any of those papers," he countered. "I had your name taken off the mortgage years ago and none of the letters are ever addressed to you just to your Mum and me AND it's not down to me for the council's incompetence if they cannot get my date of birth right!"

Regrettably I never got the chance to confront him about his other family. My youngest brother came to see me one day to talk to me about all my revelations. He begged me to allow the girls to stay at my Mum's. My brother said that he would never let anything happen to the girls. I couldn't see how he could stop it and quietly asked, "What will you do, stay up all night at the end of their beds on guard?"

"If necessary, yes." My brother stated determinedly.

"I'm sorry," I replied sadly, "but I just can't take the risk. I told him that his Dad wasn't the man he pretended to be. I showed my brother photographs of my stepfather's Mum, brother and nephew and told him about the other children my stepfather had. My brother was visibly shaken and asked me if he could present this to my stepfather. I was torn between the love and concern I had for my brother, and my desire to show evidence to my Mum. My love for my brother won and that particular rug was pulled out from under me.

After many rows, accusations and denials, I lost touch with my family except for my youngest brother. I tried to speak to them to make it right, but it just didn't work. In their eyes I was the one totally in the wrong, and no one would hear any different. My younger brothers and sister were still living at home and so were bias toward my stepfather, besides, he was their father.

I cannot begin to describe the feelings of rejection and betrayal I felt by my Mum. The one person in the world I wanted to believe me didn't. I was convinced that she knew what had been happening to me all along, after all she encouraged time alone with my stepfather, but Mum said that she didn't know.

Knowing the unbreakable bond of love I had for each of my children, I couldn't understand how my Mum could believe every word my stepfather spoke and completely disregard everything I had said. The pain and sorrow in my heart was immense.

There were a few comments from my Mum that made me realise lot more things about her. One in particular, was when she said that she would never have hurt her Mum by telling her such things. I found out that my aunt (her sister) had been abused by my Grandfather and she thought that my Mum had been also.

I was struggling with life, I'd had three children very close together, one of whom had died, I was very depressed and taking medication for it and all this had massive implications on our sex life. It had been non-existent for many months. I hoped that my Mum would understand when I said to her, "How do you think it makes me feel when my husband approaches me in bed and all I see is your husbands' face?"

"Block it out!" she snapped.

My Mum had grown up in a household where her Dad ruled, whatever he said happened without question, there was no room for debate. She married my stepfather who was a man very much like her own father. If she had admitted what kind of a man he was and what he had done to me, at least two things would cause her so much trauma, pain and suffering that she wouldn't have been able to cope: Firstly she would have to admit that she had failed to protect her daughter from living the same traumatic life she had done. I'm sure that she must have sworn to herself (as I did with my children) that she would protect her children at all costs. Actually knowing what had happened must have caused her so much pain in remembering her own pain, as well as the feelings of failure for not protecting her daughter. Secondly she could not possibly have stayed married to my stepfather if she had admitted what had been going on, but then what would she have done instead?

Mum, even to this day, needs someone to look after her and is afraid to be left alone. In my stepfather, she had met a man who was prepared to take on her and another man's children. He was willing to look after them all, feed and clothe them. My Mum couldn't see her needs ever being met if she found herself alone with even more children.

There had been a man since my Dad and before my stepfather, who wanted to marry Mum. He had not wanted me and my two sisters and demanded that we stay with her parents. Mum had refused to do it, sacrificing her chance of happiness with a man so that she could keep her children.

Mum couldn't have lived with herself if she'd admitted she knew what was happening. I still believe that deep down she did know because there were too many incidents of me being left alone with or sent to my stepfather by my Mum for her not to have known. But, if she didn't allow herself to acknowledge it, she could keep herself from actually knowing what was going on and protect herself from such an unbearable and intense pain. I suppose she just "blocked it out."

I felt angry and hurt, but also abandoned, let down and devastated, that my Mum didn't believe me or try to help me at all. My heart cried out in desperation. Desperation for my Mum to acknowledge what had happened, take me in her arms and soothe me better, and because I understood the weakness and helplessness my Mum must have felt, the regret, the failure, the memories it must have brought back for her.

So where did that leave me? Counselling, anti-depressants and despair. Donald's parents were good to me and helped out when they could and I had a close friend who was also very good to me.

Then I realised what the real emptiness was. We had joined a church but went very irregularly and the last time I went, about nine months previously, I had walked out calling God a very bad name for letting me lose Gabrielle. I decided to go back. I didn't know many people there, but an image of a ladies face came to my mind. I gave God an ultimatum, "That lady who asked if I could take mince pies to the Christingle once, I think I could talk to her. If you send her to me, I will go back to church. If not that's the end of it!"

Off I went but this lady didn't approach me, but at "the peace" the new vicar's wife introduced herself instead, "Hello, my name's Linda." She stretched out her hand for me to shake it. "Are you new or just visiting?"

"No I've been here for years just not for a few months!" I snapped abruptly, annoyed that she was even speaking to me let alone the fact that she thought I was new!

"Oh I see," Linda continued smiling, "Do you have children?"

"Yes three. One's dead, the others are in the Sunday School."

"How old are they?"

If I had been her I think I'd have quit ages ago, but she pressed on extending the hand of friendship. Her three children were around the same ages as ours. At the end of the service, I stormed home. "Ok, You've got one more chance," I ranted to God. "I'll go back once more but if that lady doesn't come to me – that's your lot!"

The following week I was reading the news sheet when I heard, "Hello Jeany, I've not seen you for a long time. May I sit with you?" My jaw dropped to the floor in amazement and I knew I had to keep my end of the bargain.

June befriended me and was instrumental in teaching me that God was a loving Father. He did love me and I was worthy of His love. To me a Father was not good, one left me, the others abused me, but God wasn't like them – He loved me!

Chapter 22

How Could I Ever Forgive?

"Forgive him! I can't and won't forgive him. Why should I? I don't want him to become a Christian and go to heaven either. I want him to rot in hell! It's not alright." I exclaimed when Linda explained that forgiveness was part of the Christian message. She had now become my best friend and we got together regularly to talk and pray.

"Forgiveness isn't about letting your stepfather get away with it or making what he did alright, it is about releasing yourself from the bitterness that is dominating your life." Linda explained.

"But I don't want to forgive him! And," I shouted angrily to Linda and John, "it's not fair that if he confesses and becomes a Christian, particularly on his death bed, that he will go to heaven which is where I hope to go. I want him to suffer and be punished with an eternity in hell."

"Well," began John, "I don't hold much stock to death bed declarations of faith. In my experience they are not always genuine, but born out of fear of death. Even if that did happen, when we are all in heaven, none of the issues you are facing now, in the past or in the future will matter. You need to forgive to move on and be released from the chains that are binding you."

Eventually, with Linda and John, I began the process of forgiveness and wrote a letter to God. I expressed the beginnings of forgiving my stepfather, however, it was nowhere near complete, just enough to start me feeling a little less bitter, depressed and tied up in knots.

Another lady in the church was an artist. Whilst we were on a Parish weekend retreat, she made a representation of my life out of rocks, stones, leaves etc. It started with a small stone bound tightly with string, the string moved to another slightly bigger stone, with less string, and then gradually moving to a large stone in the centre with no string binding it at all. The first stone was surrounded by crumpled brown leaves which gradually moved into being soft green leaves and blooms of flower and colour. "You started here," Ann explained taking my hand, "the smallest stone completely bound up with your life crumpling around you, ultimately you will become the stone in the middle, strong, tall, beautiful and free. I would suggest that you are about here at the moment." Ann pointed to a stone just under half way. Linda photographed it for me and to this day it is in a frame in my study to keep me reminded of that prophecy.

Linda and John moved on to another Parish. I was devastated to lose them and I continued to need anti-depressants and counselling. I had always admired Mary, the lady in charge of music at church. One day she approached me smiling and said, "Every now and again, a light travels around the church and lands on someone and today it's landed on you!"

"Oh yes," I answered, "why's that then?"

"Don't look so nervous – it's a good thing! I'd like you to come and join the music group and play your keyboard with me at the evening service on the first Sunday each month."

My jaw dropped to the floor. "I don't think I'm good enough for that yet."

"Trust me you are. Come along on to practice on Wednesday and see."

On Wednesday evening I walked in to the church and sat listening to the group finish the morning practice. Mary smiled at me. It was always refreshing and encouraging to watch Mary play; she really enjoyed herself and put her all in to it. Some of the morning group packed away their instruments and Mary looked up at me. "Come on then Jeany, you can't play from there. Are you going to get your keyboard out of the bag?" I shook my head and couldn't move – a spot on the carpet was my focus. Mary came to me, knelt down and held my clasped hands in hers, "What's up?"

"I can't do it; I'm not as clever as all the others. I've not been playing for very long and I just can't!" Tears began to roll down my cheeks and I was aware that the rest of the group was wondering what on earth was wrong with me.

Mary rested her forehead against mine, increasing her grip on my hands. "Okay, first of all you are more than good enough, secondly, how long you have been playing isn't what matters here it's God's anointing that counts and thirdly, it doesn't matter what anyone else thinks. Promise me one thing?"

"What's that?"

"You'll join us tonight, enjoy yourself and if you don't want to come on Sunday evening you don't have to."

"Okay." I sniffed. I played every first Sunday evening of the month, gradually turning my volume up so that people could actually hear me.

A few years later I was chatting to Mary on the telephone, eventually I told her that I must go because I needed to get packing for another Parish weekend. As requested, Donald had got me an extra suitcase from the loft before he'd gone to work, it felt heavy. I opened it and immediately rang Mary back. "Talk to me."

"Ok, well err," I had taken her by surprise. "I am putting my pansies in pots in the front garden, there will be a lovely array of colours when they are all in bloom." Mary rambled on while I remained silent. "As you know my favourite flowers are daffodils, but they are finished now."

She continued rambling on and after a while asked, "So why am I talking to you?"

"The suitcase I have just opened contains all Gabrielle's clothes and other special items I had kept. I knew that there was a case in the loft with

them in, however, I didn't realise that I would be opening that case today."
I choked.

"Ok," Mary continued, "Put them in a bag and put them to one side.
When you come back from the weekend, I will come round and help you
to do something with them. I don't know what, but it won't entail putting
them back into the loft in that case for you to come across them like this
again."

True to her word, we got together, I had covered a cardboard box in
baby paper and we sorted through all the items. I talked about each item,
and shared many memories of Gabrielle with Mary. Some items we threw
away because they just weren't worth keeping, others I kept and decided
that they would go in the same suitcase as the special items I had kept for
Megan and Elizabeth, the rest we put in the decorated box and I donated
them to a couple under financial strain who had lost a son and now had
a daughter. They were very grateful and sent me a photograph of their
daughter with a thank you note.

Mary also arranged for me to see another counsellor and for the church
to pay for the sessions. The organisation this Counsellor worked for was
in another town, it was financed by churches and all the counsellors were
Christians, but no one would have known this by just attending sessions.
The difference between this and secular counselling was that as Christians
the counsellors prayed before and after sessions but non-Christian clients
would never know this.

This last batch of counselling was the most difficult of all. I re-lived
every episode of abuse I had suffered, I spent much of the time cowering,
wrapped up in my shawl, living the fear, pain and suffering I had so long
denied. Jade was wonderful and gave me what just I needed. At first when
I heard her move in her chair I was terrified, when I felt her hand touch
my arm I withdrew, how could she touch me? I was soiled, disgusting, not

worth even liking, and yet I wanted her to hold me, to tell me that it was alright.

Jade did all of those things and more. She cried with me, held me, reassured me and above all believed me. She enabled me to see that these things did happen to me, but that none of it was my fault. I wasn't the one to blame in any way and that even if I had thrown myself at my stepfather in the first place, begging for a relationship, he was the adult and I was the child – he was the one in control. Jade wasn't suggesting for one minute that I had done this, but needed to illustrate the point as to who was the one to blame. In the same way I talked about Gabrielle, I acknowledged the pain I had tried to bury. Jade looked at all my photographs and talked with me about all the things Gabrielle used to get up to all the happy times as well as the heartache.

At last the barriers began to break down and I had admitted that all this had happened to me, not to someone else. I lived it all for the first time in my life and through the counselling was able to put it all into perspective and find some peace. I had now moved even more steps forward than I had before without taking one step forward and half a dozen back. I was free, happy and my life had turned around so I walked around the next corner.

Chapter 23

Turning The Corner

What a corner! A few years later whilst on Parish Holiday, Megan was violently sick and had a raging temperature all night. She didn't seem to pick up afterwards either and the hundred or so people there were very worried about her. She was very lethargic and didn't want to eat anything. I assumed that she was afraid to eat in case she became sick again.

A few days later I was ironing a few items before Megan came home from school. The telephone rang, it was the school to say that Megan was unwell so could I go up to the school. Panic gripped me, I thought that she must be vomiting again. I called up the stairs to Donald and Elizabeth, "I'm going to the school to pick Megan up – she's not well." I slammed the door as I rushed out.

I felt as though I was in a parallel world as I drove to the school. I saw some of Megan's friends walking along the road and remember thinking that they looked okay, and besides, it was home time so how could she be unwell? I bounced up the curb as I parked outside the school and rushed to the reception. When I got there a lady was waiting for me, "Hi Mrs Pavett, my name's Karen and I'm the school's first aider," we walked as she talked and she took me through the coded door.

Now I was really panicking, we weren't normally invited through that door. All along I had expected to find Megan with her head in a bucket, vomiting, but now I was petrified. "Megan has had some kind of fit, I've called an ambulance..." her voice was fading – I saw the ambulance – I began to run – even though I didn't know where I was going – all I knew was that I wanted to get to my beloved daughter and see she was ok. I assumed Megan had passed out in the same way I used to when I was a teenager and that once I got there, she'd see me, we'd cuddle and she'd be ok. This was not the case; Megan was in a full seizure. She was lying on a classroom floor with the Paramedics in attendance. I looked into Megan's eyes, "Mummy's here, Megan. It's ok. I'm here."

There was no recognition of me in her eyes. Her body racked violently, she was making strange noises, yelling incomprehensibly and loudly, her limbs spastic. Megan had been sitting in her maths lesson when she fell into the lap of the lad sitting next to her. He'd raised his hand, "Miss I think there's something wrong with Megan." Then she began convulsing. The pupils all left the classroom and help was called.

I tried to ring Donald to let him know what was happening but I couldn't get the words out so Karen did it for me. He told me he would call his parents to come over and then he and Elizabeth would meet me at the hospital. The paramedics struggled to get Megan onto the stretcher; she was thrashing so violently that she almost threw herself off many times and they couldn't strap her down. Karen came in the ambulance with me and we went to A & E. The school was next door to the hospital but it still seemed to take an age to get there because we had to go so slowly.

We rang our new vicar, Peter, who said he'd meet us at A & E. Megan just did not stop seizing. For her safety, the sides were up on her bed to stop her from falling off, but she was battering herself on them, she was incontinent, and her clothes had to be cut off, and trying to get a sample of blood and put lines into her veins was an impossible task as she struggled so violently. It took several of us all our strength just to keep her on the bed.

Megan was thirteen and so a Paediatric Consultant was called over from the Children's Hospital. He gave her drugs to stop the seizure but they didn't work. We were asked a barrage of questions. I didn't think she could have taken any drugs, but it was always possibility because an hour later the seizure just wasn't stopping.

I wanted Donald with me but only one of us was allowed in the Resuscitation Room at a time so most of the time it was me with Donald, his parents and Elizabeth in the Day Room, however, Peter, as our vicar, was able to stay in the resuscitation room with me as my support. Eventually, when nothing seemed to be working to bring Megan out of her seizure, one of the doctors decided to perform a CT scan. "This scan," he explained, "will show us if everything is still in the right place. It works like this. Suppose I scanned your lounge, it would show me if say, the television had fallen over, but it wouldn't show me if there was something wrong inside the television set. We just want to see if there is anything obvious."

I tried to absorb everything he was telling me. "The thing is," he continued, "Megan as you know, is very mobile and she will have to be completely still for the scan so we will have to ventilate and sedate her. If you wait in the relatives room I'll come and get you when we are back."

We all sat in the room and waited. After what seemed like an eternity, there was a knock on the door. "Mr. & Mrs. Pavett?" the doctor peered around the door. "Hi, yes, we've completed the scan and the good news is that the CT showed that everything seems to be in its place but it does mean that we are no further forward at this stage in finding out what is causing Megan to fit. Unfortunately, when we tried to bring her off the ventilator she wasn't breathing on her own and so we have had to keep her sedated. As you know, we don't have paediatric intensive care here so we are now going to ring around the London hospitals and find an intensive care bed for Megan. I'll keep you posted every step of the way. You can go back to her in 'resuss' now if you want to."

Eventually, in the middle of the night, Megan was transferred to Children's Intensive Care in London. Friends drove Donald and I there, Donald's parents took Elizabeth home with them and Peter went back to ask everyone in our church to pray.

Lots of possibilities were mentioned, meningitis, a virus, drugs, epilepsy, but they really didn't know what it was. Many tests were carried out and more blood samples were taken for analysis.

In the early hours of the morning a doctor came to us and said, "Let's go down to the relative's room." My heart sank. There was that ten ton truck again, pushing me over the sheer drop of the cliff top then landing on top of me. The last time a doctor had uttered those words it was to say that there was no hope that our daughter would survive and to give us the option of turning off the ventilator or just waiting for her to die.

Here we were again. I couldn't speak; once again I felt sick and wanted to bring up my insides. Surely I couldn't lose another of my babies? Why? What was going on? I shook from head to toe as the doctor began to talk to us. "We don't know what is causing Megan to seize but we do know that her brain is swollen. We call it Encephalitis. It's probably due to a virus, but we can't say for sure." His words were fading as I shook uncontrollably. "We will wait and see what happen for the rest of the night.....you should try to get some sleep......we will try to turn the sedation off.........see if she will wake up and breathe for herself tomorrow." The relief that enveloped me was overwhelming and I began to cry. I told the doctor what had happened the last time a doctor had taken us to the relatives' room and he was most apologetic for the situation we had just found ourselves in. From that moment on, the doctors and nurses were all told that our first daughter had died fourteen years ago and they treated us with extra special care.

Trying to prize me away from Megan's bedside was impossible. I would not leave her unless it was absolutely necessary. "Mummy's here, darling." I stroked her hair. It was stiff and needed a wash from vomit, she stank but I lay my head beside her on the bed. "I love you babe. I'm here and I'm not leaving you. Please wake up. Please be alright. I love you so much."

I spoke to Elizabeth on the telephone, my 'baby' was at home without me, in her last year of primary school, just about to take her SATs Tests and I was worried about her. These exams would be the yard mark for her moving up to Secondary school. "Hello darling, are you ok?" I struggled to get any words out.

"Hello Mummy, I'm fine don't worry about me. How's Megan?" She seemed so grown up. I tried not to cry.

"She's still asleep at the moment, Daddy's with her so that I could come and speak to you. We don't know how long it will take her to wake up or what she will be like when she does."

"She'll be okay." She reassured. Could this be an eleven year old speaking?

"I love you darling and really miss you but I'd better get back to Megan now. I don't want her to come round and me not be there. I'll see you later when Nannie and Grandad bring you up."

"Yes. I love you Mummy. Bye for now." Pain tore through my wretched body. I kept my lips tightly shut and tried to inhale my sobs so as not to let them go. I don't know if I could have stopped if I'd let myself cry.

Megan gradually woke up and tried to breathe for herself. They removed the ventilator and she began to move without fit activity which was very encouraging. She looked at me and I dared to speak to her. Would she recognise me, she hadn't the last time I spoke to her? "Hello darling, it's Mummy. Can you hear me? Do you know who I am?" She nodded. My heart leapt with joy – Megan knew me. Megan had little control over her limbs. They were too heavy for her to lift and seemed to have a mind of their own. Megan had no co-ordination. "Mummy's here, did you feel me hugging you?"

"Yes," she whispered, "and God." I cried.

I cried with relief that Megan had woken and knew me. I cried with happiness that Megan had known my hugs and had felt God hugging her, too.

The hospital provided us with B & B accommodation. Donald's parents looked after Elizabeth while Donald and I stayed in London with Megan and they all came to see us every day. Once Megan was out of intensive care we were no longer eligible for the B & B room, but one of us could stay in her room with her. Donald went home to look after Elizabeth and I stayed.

Megan was still 'all over the place'. She wouldn't settle and definitely wouldn't sleep. Her body was one big bruise from the violence during her seizure and from the fact that she had so many needles and lines put into her body. She had no suitable veins left.

Meningitis was ruled out and she was given steroids and anti-viral medication to bring the swelling down in her brain. After two weeks she was discharged to our local children's hospital. They thought that it must have been a virus which would settle down with the medication.

I wasn't happy to leave hospital because Megan wasn't right, she clung to me like a toddler, I couldn't leave the room without her getting upset and agitated.

We realised that Megan had lost memory; we worked out from what she could recall that she had lost around the last eight to nine months. She remembered being at secondary school but could only remember her first year there and not her second. Her short term memory was also very bad; I had to tell her things over and over again because she couldn't retain the information. I don't know what was worse, Megan being sedated and not knowing if she would ever wake up or seeing this stranger before me.

I rang my friend Rachel. To begin with our relationship was parent/school secretary but over the years we had become close and had shared so much. "Hello Jeany, how are you?" Her soothing voice on the other end of the phone made it hard for me to keep control.

"I dunno." Was all I could manage.

"You know we are all thinking about you. So many people are sending you their love. No-one can believe what has happened." My tummy jerked and short gasping breaths came through my nostrils as I tried to remain composed so that I could speak to Rachel but the pain was so great.

"If there is anything I can do please just say." Rachel continued. "Don't worry about Elizabeth; we're all keeping a close eye on her."

"Thanks. Can I speak to her; I just need to hear her voice."

"Of course mate. I'll go and get her for you."

Elizabeth seemed so much older than her eleven years and had a very mature head on her shoulders. I was racked with guilt. "Hello Mummy, what's up?"

"Nothing, I .... I wanted to... I just wanted hear your voice. I love you so much darling."

"I know and I love you too, Mummy. I'll be there when I've finished school. How's Megan today?"

"There's no change really. We just have to wait and see."

"Oh ok. I'm sure she'll get better soon."

"Yes, I'm sure she will. You'd better go back to class now. I'll see you later then. I love you with all my heart."

"Me too! See you later. Bye bye."

"Bye I love you." I whispered, hugging the telephone even after Elizabeth had hung up. Somehow it brought her closer to me.

One of my brothers brought my Mum and stepfather up to see Megan one day. They found it very hard and my stepfather was visibly shaken. When he left, he put his hand on my shoulder and said, "She'll be alright, please God." I was too numb even to react to his touch. I didn't see them again although we sent texts to them to keep them up to date with Megan's situation.

Megan didn't go back to school for a while. We went on a tour of her school so that she could begin to familiarize herself with it again, but she could still only remember her first year there. She hadn't even remembered that she'd won an award for her first year. Gradually she spent an odd lesson in school here and there but the rest of the time she was glued to my side.

Chapter 24

Oh No, Not Again!

I thought that things were beginning to settle. The day before Father's day Donald went away to work and the girls and I were going to a party. I stopped to get fuel and as I came out from the cashier Elizabeth rushed to me. "Megan's having a fit again!" she screamed.

I ran to the car. "Go and tell the man inside to ring for an ambulance." I carefully opened the passenger door and leant in to Megan. My mobile rang,

"Hi, I just wanted to let you know that I've arrived safely and am just about to go and get my dinner." It was Donald.

"I can't talk to you now, Megan's having another fit. We're at the petrol station and I'm waiting for an ambulance." As I threw my mobile down I heard Donald say that he would come back.

While I waited for the ambulance I called Donald's parents but got no answer so left a message then called my friend Rachel. She'd just bought a drink at the pub with another friend but left it there to come to take care of Elizabeth. "What exactly happened Elizabeth?" I asked as calmly as I could.

"She seemed to bang her head on the door so I asked her if she was alright," Elizabeth began, "she looked back at me and said, 'YES!' giving me a filthy look, then she just fell to one side and started to fit, so I ran in to get you."

"You did well, darling." It was so unfair that our baby had to grow up so quickly and see her sister going through all this.

Rachel and Jo arrived and took Elizabeth to one side so that I could concentrate on Megan and talking to the paramedics. Rachel said that they would come up to the hospital and stay with Elizabeth in the relatives room until either Donald or his parents arrived. I left the car keys at the garage for someone else to move it from the pumps not caring what happened to it.

The scenes from our last trip to A & E were replayed except this time Peter was away so our Curate came to the hospital to help us instead. We knew some of the team that came to pick her up from London from the last time, one of the nurses said sadly, "We were just talking about Megan, and wondering how she was doing but didn't expect to be coming up to do this again."

Megan was more violent, more agitated, more difficult and clingier than she was before. She'd also lost even more memory.

Apparently everyone is allowed one seizure in their life, but more than one needs investigating thoroughly. The morning after we had arrived, we saw a new doctor. Some of the blood samples taken last time were sent for "batch tests" – certain things are only tested when there is a batch to test. One test in particular had given cause for concern and so our family medical history was delved into. A diagnosis began to form; they suspected that Megan had Cerebral Lupus. Something in her immune system had gone wrong and instead of just attacking bugs etc., it had started to attack her brain, caused it to swell to such an extent that it caused seizures. The doctors were in consultation with a professor at another London Hospital. She advised them what initial treatment to give Megan but said that she would need more tests.

Megan didn't take kindly to the tests; this kind and gentle child had turned into a violent and abusive monster. Unfortunately, not all the tests could be completed because during one of the many times a nurse tried to get a blood sample with Megan fighting against her, she suddenly cried out, "I feel sick. I feel sick."

"Before the last seizure she told me she felt a bit sick!" panic gripped me once again.

"I FEEL SICK!" Megan shouted – then silence filled the air as she fell into another seizure. Once again I feared for her life. She didn't seem to be getting back to normal; in fact she seemed to be getting worse.

I told Donald to ring my Mum and tell them that we would pay their train fare so that they could come to see Megan. I felt that it would be the last time they would ever see her. My Mum said that they couldn't come today, but that if Megan was still in hospital at the weekend and if the pension was paid in, they would come then. Once again, when I cried for help, my Mum didn't respond.

The tests were stopped and Megan was put on steroids until her treatment could be transferred to the other London Hospital. The problem was that there were no beds available so as soon as she was stable enough, we were sent back to our local hospital. They then sent us home to wait for the call to begin Megan's treatment.

Megan began to put on lots of weight with the steroids, which meant we had to keep buying her new clothes. The financial implications were huge; the cost of train fare, fuel, meals, new clothes, magazines & DVD's to help Megan pass the time in hospital. We had no savings and so used visa cards for everything, we just didn't care how much everything cost, how much debt we created, all that mattered was life.

The treatment for Lupus was very hard. Megan had a lot of medication to take a three or four times a day and I had to take Megan to London every month for chemotherapy – at the very least it was an overnight stay. The two Consultants caring for Megan on the rheumatology ward were wonderful. They didn't tire of explaining everything and showed great care and compassion towards us all.

When they administered the chemo the nurses had to put on protective clothing so that there was absolutely no chance of them being splashed with the drugs because it was very dangerous. And yet I had to sign a consent form to have this poison put into our daughter. I was afraid when I saw it for the first time. Everything was so much more difficult because Megan's veins were all shot. She had even been burned by one of the antiviral drugs and had a crater in her ankle of dead flesh for which she was under our local burns unit to treat it. I wanted to shout at the nurses and refuse the chemo or even take it myself. From that moment on I kept thinking that I would wake up and it would all have been another nightmare.

After six months the frequency of the chemo was taken to once every three months. Megan seemed to be settling down and getting some sort of life back, but I still felt as though I was in a parallel world. Surely I would wake up and get back to reality soon? We began to relax a little as the routines became a way of life.

Megan was chosen to go on a 'holiday of a lifetime' with a company called Dreamflight. The holiday was to Disneyland Florida for a fortnight and one carer had two children to look after. British doctors and nurses went with them and were joined by American doctors and nurses when they got there.

For over a year Elizabeth had taken a back seat in our family life and had played a huge part in caring for Megan so we decided to take Elizabeth to Disneyland Paris for a few days while Megan was in America.

Even though I worried about Megan, it was wonderful to be free from the routine of drugs and medical care and to spend some quality time with Donald and Elizabeth. Elizabeth loved being with Donald and I, it was such a special time for the three of us and we really enjoyed ourselves.

At the end of Megan's holiday we queued in the aeroplane hangar to pick her up. I turned to Donald, "I think that she either has been ill or she is going to be."

"Oh for goodness sake," Donald despaired, "Why do you always have to think the worst and over-react?"

"Don't speak to me like that; I just have a gut feeling." I turned away from Donald annoyed that he wasn't taking me seriously.

Megan didn't seem very excited to see us or to have had a nice time and was very quiet. "See, I told you!" I snapped.

"She's just tired," Donald sighed, "It will have been a long busy holiday and a long flight home." Maybe Donald was right and the jet lag had worn her out. She slept a lot snuggled up with me either on the sofa or in our bed – Donald slept in Megan's bed. She seemed unsettled, had a tremor in her hands, she kept having nightmares and jerked in her sleep.

A few days later on my birthday, the girls brought me breakfast in bed and gave me cards and gifts. Megan gave me two cards; one was for a special Mum and the other a special friend. I was talking to my six year old niece on the telephone downstairs when I thought I heard something. I called up the stairs, "Megan, did you call?" No answer. "Megan, are you alright?"

Elizabeth was in her room with her door closed and radio on. I began to walk up the stairs, I wanted to run, and yet I was afraid of what I might find when I got there, everything was in slow motion. Megan was standing in the shower with a blank look on her face and making no sound. "Megan." There was no response. "Megan's not well I have to go now," I told my niece and threw the telephone to the floor. "Come on Megan, Mummy's here; let's get you out of the shower darling." As soon as I touched Megan's skin, she fell into my arms and I began to lift her dead weight over the bath. "Elizabeth! Elizabeth, take my mobile and tell Daddy to come back now!" I screeched. He'd just left for work.

I grappled for the telephone across the landing floor as I brought Megan to the ground by now in a full blown seizure – her lips turning blue. I dialled 999 but didn't seem to be getting through; my niece hadn't hung up the telephone so I could hear my sisters' voice on the other end. "Hannah was confused, Jeany, I'll hang up now"

I called the ambulance and Donald appeared at the top of the stairs, angry, "Why now? What is happening? I thought it was all sorted now – what's the treatment all been for?" He thumped the wall.

"I told you, didn't I? I told you she wasn't right and you just fobbed me off again!" I yelled.

"Yes, yes I know. You were right again and I was wrong. Happy now?" He chided.

"No, but I just wish you would listen to me when I say things instead of thinking I'm just paranoid!" I countered.

Elizabeth felt terribly guilty, "If only I'd not had my door shut and radio on I might have heard Megan call out."

"Don't worry darling, it's not your fault." I reassured her and Donald hugged her as we began to calm our anger.

I sat on the floor and I cradled Megan in my arms I and waited for the ambulance to arrive.

There was another big issue though; we were in the process of having building work done on the front of our house and which meant the Paramedics were a wary of the safety of taking Megan across the boards spanning deep footings. Donald said that he would carry her across if necessary not caring if he hurt his back or anything else – he just wanted to get her into the ambulance. The paramedics, as usual, were fantastic and said that it was okay, they would manage.

We were approximately sixteen months into her treatment and were about to have the last quarterly round of chemo before moving on to six monthly. Megan was taken to London from A & E.

This time I was really angry with God. I went and sat on the floor in the stairwell leading to Megan's ward my elbows on my knees, head resting in my hands, "You are not having another one of my children!" I shouted.

Megan's behaviour and language were absolutely appalling; she was extremely violent and rude but had no idea what she was doing or saying, she had no inhibitions and no control at all, it was heartbreaking. This lovely daughter and sister, one of the most kind-hearted and caring people you could ever wish to meet who had just given me those beautiful birthday cards, was punching, kicking and spitting at us in a deliberate and vicious manner and she had become a most hateful, rude and wicked child.

"Elizabeth, come here a minute," she said in an excited whisper from behind the bars on her bed.

"What do you want?" Elizabeth asked.

"Come here," she beckoned. Elizabeth went to Megan's side and leaned forward. Megan punched her on the nose.

There were many more times Megan was violent towards Elizabeth, like when Megan appeared to want to give Elizabeth a hug, instead she head butted her and while Elizabeth was helping Megan by taking her for a walk through the corridor, Megan shoved Elizabeth into the wall causing her to fall into a metal container on the wall stunning her and enabling Megan to escape.

I was so torn, my love for Elizabeth made my heart cry for the pain she was in and yet we all knew Megan didn't know what she was doing and was not in control of her actions. The only way I could get Megan to begin to behave was to bribe her with sweets. If she misbehaved I would tell her she couldn't have any, when she spat on the floor for example, "Now you can get out of bed and mop that up – it's very naughty of you." I told her.

"NO!"

"If you don't get out of bed and mop it up by the time I counted to three you won't have any sweets. One... two..." As I drew breath for three, Megan stomped out of bed, snatched a paper towel and bent down to mop up her spit.

"I want a sweet now!" she demanded.

I always kept my word, good or bad, "...there you are that wasn't so bad after all was it?" I gave Megan a sweet, "Now don't spit again – it's very naughty!"

Megan wanted to eat sweets all the time, even those with nuts in and she hated nuts. I didn't realise one day that she had managed to get hold of a whole box of sweets. She ate them all and threw the empty box at me; it hit me in the head which hurt me and gave rise to Megan to laughing hysterically. The fact that the box hurt me didn't matter, it was the fact that the daughter who loved me and would do anything for me, was laughing hysterically because she had hurt me.

One incident which could have proven very dangerous was when Megan had managed some good behaviour, so I kept my promise to take her in her wheelchair to the canteen so that she could choose something nice to eat. She was insistent on wheeling herself, I was equally insistent on pushing her. She chose her cake and waited until I was occupied with paying for our goods, then escaped. "Come back Megan," I was torn between paying for my goods and rushing after her.

"I'm just going to save us a table over here!" She replied in an unconvincing tone as she headed toward a vacant table.

I turned back to the cashier. The next thing I heard was, "WEEEEEEEEEEEEEE!" Megan had spotted a slope, wheeled herself

141

up to the top of it and then pushed herself off free-wheeling down. It could have been amusing, but for the pushchair at the bottom of the slope which Megan ploughed into. Fortunately the baby was in its grandmother's arms, because the pushchair went flying.

I thought that this time Megan was not going to recover and that we would be left with a mentally handicapped daughter for the rest of her life. My heart was heavy; Megan had such potential and now all that was slipping away. There were times when I just wanted to give up, but I had to keep strong for Megan and Elizabeth.

Chapter 25

A Relationship Under Strain

Donald and I argued nearly every time we saw each other. I wanted him to take me in his arms and make it all right again, to spend more time with me at the hospital but all he seemed interested in was going to work and just bringing Elizabeth up each evening. I lashed out at him verbally and when he did try to cuddle me I pushed him away. The anger inside me was so strong and I didn't know how to cope with it. I was angry because another of my daughters was critically ill, I couldn't be with both Megan and Elizabeth at the same time, Donald was concerned with going to work and I couldn't care less about it, I needed him with me. I was angry because I had been dealt such a diabolical life. My stepfather was still alive; he'd led a life of deliberately hurting and using people for his own ends. Here I was once again a frightened, lonely victim full of pain and suffering.

The doctor who looked after Nicola on the Dreamflight trip came to see her regularly and talked to her about their holiday to calm her when they were trying to put drip lines in and to help her memory. She was a fantastic support and I will be eternally grateful to her for all that she did for us.

Megan had a new course of treatment, retuximab which is another cancer treating drug, given to deplete her B cells, as well as continuing with the cyclophosphamide. She began to have occasional lucid moments – a glimmer of hope! The swelling in her brain very slowly went down and as she began to recover Megan told me that she knew that her actions were wrong but she couldn't stop herself.

Two weeks later Megan had a further course of the two drugs and they told me that this should keep everything under control. "Why didn't Megan have this treatment before?" I wondered.

"The treatment we gave Megan in the first place is usually enough to get the lupus under control." Megan's Consultant explained. "The drugs are very strong and we always like to treat with the least amount of drug possible, however, in Megan's case her lupus broke through the treatment and so she needed extra help."

"I see." I mulled this explanation over in my mind.

"We will also give Megan another oral drug called MMF to take alongside her other medication."

Since this treatment Megan has taken medication every day and has had regular check up's as an outpatient with the same consultant. When she became nineteen she had to be transferred to the adult side of the hospital, it was a sad day. We learned that many times, lupus is misdiagnosed for months or even years, which leaves the patient with many other medical issues often irreversible. We met a patient who had been misdiagnosed for two or three years and as a result had permanent problems with her spine. We thank God that the keen, young doctor picked it up after only approximately six weeks since her first seizure. They also found that Megan had an underactive thyroid.

As with Gabrielle, I found it very difficult to pray during these traumatic times and so left the praying to everyone else we knew, as well as some people we didn't know. Gradually, I was able to give Megan into God's care, and slowly, very slowly, our Megan began to come back to us. She was horrified to learn of her behaviour, language and violence and couldn't believe she had behaved in that way. She was determined that her illness would not dominate her life. At first she objected to all the drugs she had to take each day and all the hospital check-ups, but soon they all became a way of life. Despite missing so much school and losing her memory Megan went on to achieve four A's, five B's and two C's in her GCSE's, gained part-time employment in a local shop, passed her driving test, obtained two B's a C and a D at 'A' Level and achieved many awards from school.

Chapter 26

Megan's Miracles

God has certainly looked after Megan – apart from the miracle of her life – God gave her a very special gift. I was appointed as head of worship at church when Peter took over as our vicar. I didn't have a drummer so simply looked up towards the sky one day and said, "I haven't got a drummer. Please can you send me one?"

My jaw dropped to the floor when, a few days later, Megan – in the midst of her uncontrolled illness – walked up to the drum kit and said, "I'll give it a go," and she just played. Ever since she has played in our Worship Team, each time she plays she gets better and better. It is amazing.

Megan had no intention to go to university but wanted to go straight out to work. I felt confident that God had plan for her and told her that she could take the whole of the summer off before rushing into full time work.

As soon as September came Megan decided to go to an office agency she'd heard was good, however, found she couldn't get in because it was a coded door lock. A lady was outside and asked Megan if she could offer her any assistance. Megan explained her intentions.

"Well I work for the agency upstairs from them and I think I have just the job for you. It is temporary until Christmas, but could become permanent. The only thing is that it is a Christian organisation and they say prayers each morning; although you won't have to join in if you don't want to."

"I don't have an issue with that because I am a Christian!" Megan was amazed how everything fitted together. Megan began working there and took a leap of faith by giving up her part-time job in the shop even though she was afraid that she'd be left with nothing at Christmas. After a couple of months the company decided to advertise Megan's job and she was invited to apply for it. It didn't take long before Megan became their full-time, permanent Administrator.

Elizabeth's mind has been set on going into medicine for many years now. Despite everything that Megan put her through, Elizabeth remained calm and caring. Originally, she wanted to go into nursing, but changed her mind and decided that she'd like to go into Midwifery instead. It is a profession where her caring nature and huge heart will be well placed. Despite the trauma in her life, she has remained focused at school, and has constantly achieved high marks and has been accepted into our local university to train to be a Midwife – her hearts' desire.

During all the time that Megan was ill, so was I. I was losing copious amounts blood every day but refused to be taken in for a hysterectomy until Megan was better. Unfortunately, I got to a point when I had lost so much blood that I was in danger of exsanguination (bleeding to death). I had just struggled up to the hospital in London with Megan for one of her chemotherapy sessions, only to find that I had to return home urgently for a blood transfusion before they could perform my hysterectomy. I waited for Donald to come to London to be with Megan before I would leave for my own hospital back home.

The months following my operation were the hardest for me to cope with because I physically could not take care of our girls. Donald's parents came over to help me and to make sure that I didn't do anything and friends also came round to offer help. I was eternally grateful to them; however, I did find it incredibly difficult to accept help from anyone. I wanted to do it myself, but because I had been so ill before the operation, it took me longer to recover after it. I was physically and emotionally drained.

Chapter 27

How was I Able to Cope?

How did I cope with so much tragedy? Why me? How did I survive? What's more, how can I believe in God? To answer every question I have ever asked myself, and others have asked of me, I want to go back to the experiences I didn't understand at church when I was younger. Through the counselling and friends, I understood what it all was and why I was so drawn to the church. How was I able to remain steadfast and strong about going to church when in everything else, I had caved in to the demands made by my stepfather.

It explains how, despite everything, I once again have a relationship with my family. Some members are closer to me than others, but I have to accept that for the others, I will never have the relationship I crave, but at least I have some sort of relationship with them all. Since the meeting Donald and I had when I confronted my Mum and stepfather with what had happened to me as a child the subject has never been spoken about or acknowledged again. I kept on going back to see my family even though I felt even more hurt and rejection with each visit and it was against the advice of many of my friends. However I never wanted to see my stepfather or acknowledge him and I was relieved if he was out when I visited my Mum. I stopped sending him father's day or birthday cards and at Christmas would not send 'Mum & Dad' cards to them both. I just couldn't bring myself to do it because I felt it would be two faced. This caused more issues with my family. Mum told me that they were a package, if I wanted her and I had to accept him.

Those early experiences explain how I had the courage to find my Dad and begin a relationship with him. At first it was difficult. The first time we met, Elizabeth was under a year. We met up in a country park. I recognised him instantly, I knew my Dad, I felt the bond that the years could not take away. He looked in the car at the girls, Elizabeth's nose was running, he took his handkerchief from his pocket and cleaned it for her. My heart and mind leaped back in time.

To him I was still his little girl, whom he had missed desperately; he'd never stopped loving me and regretted all the absent years. He wanted to hug me, sit next to me with his arm around me but I just wasn't comfortable with that at all.

We had so much to learn about each other. Dad never once blamed my Mum for their marriage break up. He accepted total responsibility for it and he had so many regrets. When he learned about my stepfather he had even more regrets and he struggled to come to terms with what had happened to me. He'd thought that we were one big happy family and after trying to make contact with us on many occasions, felt it best to leave us to get on with our lives, besides it wasn't easy to travel two hundred miles in those days.

Dad had always been a Christian, but he just couldn't bring himself to say the part of the Lord's Prayer where it talks about forgiving others. Dad had never experienced God as a reality in his church and each time he came to my church, he would always walk out of the service part way through and return at the end. He said it was because he was overcome with emotion. One day he told me that he was going to find a church like mine where he lived, a church alive with the Holy Spirit; that encourages a relationship with God the Father.

He prayed and felt drawn to a church where he settled very quickly and found God in a very real and positive way leading to his full immersion and Holy Spirit baptisms and being able to say the Lord's Prayer in full – and mean it.

You see, God saw how awful we humans had become, we turned away from Him, we became very self-centred, jealous, greedy, murderous … the list is endless, and because we were so sinful, God – Perfect God – couldn't be near us, He cannot touch sin, so He came to earth in human form as Jesus Christ, and taught us how we should live, then He died for us, He was whipped, beaten, ridiculed and hung on a cross, to pay the price of all our sin. He was buried, but God did not abandon Him, He raised Him to life and took Him back into heaven but sent the third part of the Trinity to help us, the Holy Spirit.

Now many dispute the existence of God, some say that there is a "higher force", or that all religions point to the same God. Still others believe that there is some sort of God, but dispute Jesus Christ and the Holy Spirit. The fact that Jesus Christ lived on this earth is documented in the history books written at that time, other religious books, as well as the Bible. Despite all claims to the contrary God himself says that the only way to Him, is through His Son, Jesus Christ.

Many believe that the Bible is rubbish, but I have learned that if you study it rather than read it, understand what life was like at the time it was written, then you realise the truths it contains. But what no one can dispute is my experiences. Those very early experiences I felt way back in childhood I now know, was God's Holy Spirit. I forgot the pain and trauma all the time I was in church with those warm, tingly feelings, it was as if I was in another world – a safe world. When I prayed at home or read the Bible, I had those same protective feelings.

I cannot quote many verses from the Bible, I am not knowledgeable about the history of it, the science of the world and universe, but I do know the power and strength I have felt to cope with the situations in my life. I don't look for what isn't there, the "How?" "Why?" or "What for?"

God is my loving Father. He grieves when I grieve, rejoices when I rejoice and He is always close by my side. When I don't feel that He is there, it is because I have pushed Him away and tried to hide or cope by myself. His only Son suffered and died a horrible, tortuous death for the vilest of people as well as for the good.

God gave Jesus Christ for me, yes Jesus came for all of us, but He also came just for me. He suffered ridicule, He was let down by His friends, He was beaten and abused, separated from His Father. God the Father and God the Son were reunited when He rose from the dead and ascended into heaven. God the Holy Spirit, counsellor, comforter, strengthener, guide, healer, friend came to earth for me.

When we call on God, He answers, it is not always the answer we want but then which good father gives their children everything they ask for? God didn't stop these things from happening to me, He wasn't – and isn't ever – responsible for other peoples' actions, He leaves us to make our own decisions. We are not puppets, we have freewill. We are living on earth not in heaven and we have heaven to look forward to.

Life taught me not to rely or trust anyone. Life is cruel, harsh, wicked and at times not worth living. Each time I developed a 'best friend'/confidant and built up the courage to pour out my heart when I was hurting, the friendship ended because they moved away and I was left once again with feelings of devastation and betrayal. Many times I decided that I would manage on my own and not take anyone into my confidence ever again. But God even helped here.

God has taught me that there is a way forward, I can live life to the full, and through all my experiences, I can help other people to come through their trials and traumas, there is hope for life, hope for eternity and that there are good and trustworthy people in this world.

I had heard that in the Bible it says that when you bless your enemies it is like heaping hot, burning coals on their heads. I spent many times "blessing" my stepfather but still felt bitter and unforgiving, until one day I realised the truth.

My brother lost a baby son and we had his funeral at the crematorium. As we walked out to look at the flowers, my stepfather (a frail old man in his eighties) stumbled. I instinctively put out my hand to steady his fall. At that moment he let out a sob, it was as though a bolt of electricity had passed through us and I realised that my simple action had both blessed him and heaped hot coals on his head at the same time. Furthermore, my stepfather was admitted into hospital with pneumonia and a blockage causing jaundice. As a result of the treatment he contracted a super bug which meant that he had to have an operation to remove a portion of his gut and would be left with a colostomy bag. He had a fifty-fifty chance of surviving the operation and certain death if he didn't have it – he was very sick.

After surviving the operation he seemed to be doing well until he contracted another super bug and treatment for the blockage dragged him down. He began to vomit blood so much that he eventually had to be ventilated and sedated. After investigations and tests we were invited to gather in the relatives room by the doctor where he told us that my stepfather was very, very sick. He had the two superbugs as well as all the other medical issues and had lost a considerable amount of blood and they couldn't stop the bleeding in his stomach.

The Doctor went through the notes from the first time my stepfather had been admitted and talked about all the things that were wrong with him. Then came those words, "... and bearing in mind he is in his eighties, and all that is wrong with him, the kindest thing now is to decide when to stop treatment. We cannot stop the bleeding in his stomach and we don't know what other complications the blood loss has caused. The machine is breathing for him and we have medically done all that we can – all that's left is to keep him comfortable. I'll leave you alone now but please do come and see me if there is anything else you'd like to know." My Mum was devastated; she clung to me screaming and crying and would not accept what the doctor had just said. She declared that if he died, she didn't want to live either.

I went out to find the doctor. "Excuse me Doctor. I have been in this position before with my daughter and we had to turn her life support off so I understand that you don't say these things lightly, but my Mum won't accept that he is never going home again. Is this the very end of the line? Is my stepfather definitely going to die?"

"Yes. Your Mum will have to accept it because there is nothing more we can do. As I said just now, bearing in mind his age and all that is wrong with him, the kindest thing is to decide when to stop treatment." I should have been jumping up and down for joy – at last he would be punished, I would be free and rid of him. However, I wasn't. I could see how devastated my Mum was and how she felt her life had ended and my heart leapt out to her. I asked my church family to pray for him and when I prayed I felt as though I had been 'transported' to a court room.

I saw God as judge, my stepfather in the dock and I was the lawyer. I pleaded with God not to let my stepfather die this way. I wanted to give him the opportunity to realise the actions of his life, to apologise and to make his peace with God. I desperately didn't want him to 'rot in hell' as I had done for so many years and I wanted the opportunity to testify to him and to my family, that God had saved his life.

Miraculously the bleeding stopped, my stepfather woke from the sedation and after several months of treatment and rehabilitation he went home. Praise God for his healing!

Throughout the ordeal Mum and I spent a lot of time together. I tried to go to see her every day although some days it was difficult because of my own commitments and we lived over twenty miles away from each other. We had lunch out, I took her to and from the hospital and care home, she even came to my house on the May Bank holiday for dinner which I was thrilled about. Despite the situation being so dire, it was wonderful to spend so much time with my Mum as it was the first time for many years.

I regularly visit my family now and Donald often does DIY jobs for them that my stepfather can no longer manage. I have not received any kind of apology, I have witnessed to him and who knows what is in his mind? I do know, that I can sit in the same room as him, talk to him, I can kiss his cheek to bid him farewell, and do you know what? I feel so much better for it. I am not bound up; bitter and twisted as I was when I constantly wished him dead. Yes, it is still sometimes very hard, yes, I have to re-forgive him time and again, yes, it is unfair that I have suffered so much and yes, there are times when I take a dip downwards again, perhaps someone will say or do something, quite innocent, but for me it will bring back an awful memory and I can easily become withdrawn and angry but I cannot bring myself to upset them by telling them how much they have upset me. I offer the situation to God, and seek to always have a very good friend to pray for me and I soon come back up again and I remember all the good things I have in my life which shows me that God has always been there even when I didn't know it.

Chapter 28

A Moment of Thanks

I am thankful for Donald. My life could have turned out so differently if I had not had the love of a good man. I could have found myself caught up in a spiral of men similar to my stepfather, or I could have turned away from men altogether. Though there have been many periods during our marriage where intimacy has been a major issue for me and very likely this will happen again at times, but, God has restored, and rebuilt that side of my life too – and I couldn't want for more.

I am thankful to God for Gabrielle's life, no matter how short it was. I know that would go through it all again – even if the outcome was the same.

I am thankful for Megan and Elizabeth, they make my life complete and I would lay down my life for them.

I am thankful for all those people I don't even know about, who, through their dedication and commitment, made medicine what it is, as well as those I do know who cared for our daughters and me for so many years. I remember each one of them and all that they have done.

I am thankful that I have been a part of two warm and caring churches before and during our marriage. The more I let my defences down, the more I realise that people do care about me, I am loved by them and they want to help me.

I am thankful to Donald's family for all the support and love they have given me over the years, for being there when I needed them and for all the washing, ironing, housework as well as emotional support.

I am thankful for all those special people in my life who have helped me to rebuild it, which has enabled me to be in the place I am today. I remember them all every day and thank God that they came into my life no matter how long or short a time it was for.

I am thankful to all those who encouraged me to write this book, for their excitement and commitment to helping me get it out into the world.

Here's the big one! I am truly thankful to my Mum. I don't blame her or accuse her; I understand and know the fear she has lived in all her life and how very difficult it is to break a cycle that has become normality. For many years I couldn't do it and there was safety in living a life I knew no matter how awful it was, and absolute fear in stepping out into a new life. I was so much more fortunate than my Mum I was able to find the way out. My prayer now is that one day my Mum will be released from her hurts and find her way out. I love my Mum desperately and will for eternity. This book has never been intended to hurt my family which is why names are changed – to protect them.

I would never have believed I would reach the position I am in today. No matter what my exterior showed, inside I was a frightened, no I was absolutely petrified; an abused child with no confidence and no self-esteem, who wanted to hide away in a dark corner from the world. As an adult, after having children, I wanted to sit and stare at the blank walls all day, to disappear, retreat into my own world and never come out.

I am now a successful woman; a music teacher with most pupils achieving "Distinctions" in their exams and an Administrator. Not only that, I am the Musical Director of worship at church, have been elected Church Warden and now I'm a published author. I have told my story as I have lived it, felt it and interpreted it.

I don't say that I am totally confident in everything I do. I am still nervous; doubt my abilities and credibility sometimes. I still have times when I worry about Donald and our girls finding someone better than me.

But, if I remain focused on my gifts, achievements and on God who has given me the strength I've needed to cope throughout my life, I know that anything is possible.

Without God by my side I would have been nothing and I could never have made it through. Despite all that has happened I know that He is in control. I gave up asking, "Why?" a long time ago. There are still times I still say that it is not fair; but then I have to accept God's grace to help me through and I call on one of the close friends He has given me for a hug, prayer and fellowship.

There are many times I have wanted to "throw the towel in". But when I was so desperate for help that I cried out to God from the pit of my stomach, He answered me. He gave me some very special people to care for me over a number of years. Some of those people are not in my circle of friends now, some are but their lives have moved on and so we are not close anymore. They obeyed their calling from God, and that enabled me to be set free. I am eternally grateful to all those people God used as channels to help to pick me up and start again.

Over the years when people have prayed for me, God has revealed Bible verses for me. They have helped to transform my life and so I have listed them in the following pages.

I have also included the letter I wrote to Gabrielle shortly after she died. It is a letter that was written full of heartache, but writing it gave me comfort. I still think of Gabrielle every time I hear those 'certain songs', sometimes with sadness but sometimes with joy.

This book was "under construction" for twenty-two years. It began when I kept a diary during my pregnancy with Gabrielle. I felt prompted several years later to try to put it into a book. I was too afraid to enquire about the possibility of it being published, but did loan it in its earliest form to a few acquaintances who had lost babies. They told me that they felt encouraged by it.

For many years I wasn't in the position to cope if it was rejected and I felt that it was unfinished. It needed more than the story of Gabrielle, but I didn't know how to write it. I also wondered what would happen if my extended family read it. How would they feel about it?

'Life After Death' has been covered in prayer and I am ready to accept the course it is to take. I felt very strongly that this message had to 'get out there' and help others, but I didn't want to upset my family. So to protect them, I have changed names.

I pray that you are able to take hope and encouragement from what you have read and that you draw closer to God and feel His loving arms around you, just as He has been hugging me and has given me 'Life After Death'. If you are suffering, please don't be afraid to face the pain, express it and accept help so that you can move forward and begin to live.

I have always loved to express myself in the written word and through song. For me, songs and music are a passionate expression of feelings. There have been many songs over the years that I have played to Donald, and asked him to read the words to them also.

I pray that through reading this book you have found hope for tomorrow and that it has helped you, given you comfort and encouragement.

I pray that you find peace and hope, the peace and hope that only God the Father, Son and Holy Spirit can bring into your life. There are many churches where the Holy Spirit dwells powerfully, ask God to direct you and you will find Him and a family to nurture, nourish and cherish you.

In the Name of Jesus. Amen.

Thank you for reading it and may God Bless you always,
Jeany

My Letter to Gabrielle

This is the letter I wrote to Gabrielle;

Gabrielle, my darling,

My feelings can be described, using two songs by Gloria Estefan. Funnily enough one of them kept being played on the radio during your final week at the hospital where you lived for your entire short life.

"The time flies when you're having fun" – and it certainly did. Six months flew by so quickly, pushing aside the heartache; we had so much fun together, playing learning and loving.

"Hold on to every bit of hope, I heard somebody say" – Daddy and I certainly did that, we love you so much and hoped against hope that we would get you home and we could live together as any other family would.

"But I can't stay away from you, I don't wanna let you go, and though it's killing me, that's true, there's just some things I can't control." It was so hard to watch you die. There was nothing I could do. I just had to sit there and watch you "slipping through my hands", the pain, helplessness and love will never go away until the day I die and join you in Heaven.

"You're leaving me no other choice, than to turn and walk away, look over your shoulder, I'll be there, and you can count on me to stay." You left us no other choice, Gabrielle, than to let God take you and we had to walk away, but my darling that is only your physical appearance, the rest of you lives on in our hearts.

"I'll do anything for you, though you're not here, since you said we're through, it seems like years. Time keeps dragging on and on and forever's been and gone, still I can't figure what went wrong." You and God chose

159

that you'd leave us behind on this earth and you went to be with Him. I can't figure it out – it's beyond my comprehension. It's only a month since you died and it seems as though it's so long away. Time has dragged on and on.

"Don't you ever think that I don't love you, that for one minute I forgot you, but sometimes things don't turn out right, and you just have to say goodbye." – Things didn't work out right for us Gabrielle, and we had to say goodbye. I wish to God it had worked out right. I hurt more than I could ever say – there are just no words that can describe it – I long to hold you and cuddle you and see you. I've got photographs, a video and tape recording but it's you that I want darling.

Daddy and I also want a brother and/or sister for you. We are trying now, but don't you ever think that you will be forgotten because you won't. You are our first child and always will be. Subsequent children are additions to our family, not replacements. No one could ever replace you.

Don't forget we love you Gabrielle my love and we always will until we too die, and then we will all be together again.

All my love forever,

Mummy

xxxxx

Appendix B

Special Verses from The New International Version of The Bible.

"And we know that in all things God works for the good of those who love Him, who have been called according to His purpose. For those God foreknew He also pre-destined to be conformed to the likeness of His Son, that he might be the firstborn among many brothers. And those He predestined, He also called; those He called, He also justified; those He justified, He also glorified."
Romans 8 vs. 28–30 NIV

But now, this is what the Lord says –
He who created you, (O Jeany)
He who formed you, (Jeany);
"Fear not, for I have redeemed you;
I have summoned you by name; you are mine.
When you pass through the waters,
I will be with you;
and when you pass through the rivers,
they will not sweep over you.
When you walk through the fire,
you will not be burned;
the flames will not set you ablaze.
For I am the Lord, your God,
the Holy One of Israel, your Saviour;
… since you (Jeany,) are precious and honoured in My sight,
and because I love you,

I will give men in exchange for you,
and people in exchange for your life.
Do not be afraid, (Jeany) for I am with you. Isaiah 43 (I was given this passage replacing 'Israel' for my name) NIV

…being confident of this, that He who began a good work in you will carry it on to completion until the day of Christ Jesus. Philippians 1 vs. 6 NIV

Let your gentleness be evident to all. The Lord is near. Do not be anxious about anything, but in everything, by prayer and petition, with thanksgiving, present your requests to God. And the peace of God, which transcends all understanding, will guard your hearts and your minds in Christ Jesus. Philippians 4 vs. 5–7 NIV

Appendix C

A Word Given

On Easter Sunday a member of the congregation came to talk to our Music Group after the service with a vision and word of encouragement.

While we were practicing before the service, he had seen a Seraph at the back of church with its wings spread out. He told us he felt that we were about to take worship to the next level, we were united, anointed and we would see growth in the group. He also said that God had a special anointing on me and a special plan for me.

When I got home I looked up "Seraph" and found the following information to further encourage both the music group and me. In the Christian angelic hierarchy, seraphim represent the highest rank of angels. Angels of the first sphere work as heavenly guardians of God's throne.

The Seraphim (singular "Seraph") mentioned in Isaiah, serve as the caretakers of God's throne and continuously sing praises: "Holy, holy, holy is the Lord of hosts. All the earth is filled with His Glory."

It is said that there are four Seraphim surrounding God's throne, where they burn eternally from love and zeal for God. The name Seraphim means "the burning ones."

In the year that King Uzziah died I saw the Lord sitting upon a throne, high and lifted up; and his train filled the temple. Above Him stood the seraphim; each had six wings: with two he covered his face, and with two he covered his feet, and with two he flew. and one called to another and said:

"Holy, holy, holy is the Lord of hosts; The whole earth is full of His glory."

And the foundations of the thresholds shook at the voice of him who called, and the house was filled with smoke. And I said: Woe is me! For I am lost; for

I am a man with unclean lips, and I dwell in the midst of a people of unclean lips; for my eyes have seen the King, the Lord of hosts!

Then flew one of the seraphim to me, having in his hand a burning coal which he had taken with tongs from the alter. And he touched my mouth, and said: Behold, this has touched your lips; your guilt is taken away, and your sin forgiven. Isaiah 6: 1-7

The Seraphim make their first Christian appearance in the book of Revelation chapter 4 verses 6—8, where they are forever in God's presence and praising Him constantly:

"Day and night they never stop saying: 'Holy, holy, holy is the Lord God Almighty, who was, and is, and is to come.'"

The Seraphim and the Cherubim are, in Christian theology, two separate types of angels. The descriptions of the Seraphim, Cherubim and Ophanim are often similar, but still distinguishable.

When I was young I had many recurring dreams, they seemed to reflect my life. My investigations brought one of my dreams to mind. The dream happened before my life of abuse began. My dream was this:-

If I didn't get home from school by four o'clock, my house disappeared and I became a cherub and had to fly around the world all night to search for my home. Most of the time, I had my sisters on my back, carrying them with me as I flew through the night. The house was always in its usual place in the morning.

At the time I had the dream I didn't see any significance in my turning into a Cherub. The significance I did see was that in reality I had to be in from school by four o'clock or else it meant trouble. To me the dream reflected my life.

After researching Seraph (the highest ranking angel) and being told that God has a special anointing for me, I was reminded of this recurring dream. A Cherub is second in the ranking of angels. Now I'm not saying that I am an angel or a cherub, but through this word I saw something that moved me to tears. Not because it is awful, but because it is so fantastic.

It was especially significant because I had finished this book. During the course of twenty years I developed it to help others, but the last couple of weeks were particularly difficult. I felt I needed to move on to the next phase to complete the last few chapters to show God's healing hand for all to see.

I felt that the dream was confirmation that God had always had His hand on me. I believe that God gave me my own personal Cherub to protect me from harm while I was searching, lost and had nowhere else to turn.

Amen and Hallelujah.

Praise be always to the King of Kings!